Mario Calabresi has worked f[...] and for the Roman daily *La Rep[...]* aging editor and New York correspondent from 2006 to 2009. Currently he is the editor in chief of *La Stampa*, one of Italy's most influential national newspapers, headquartered in Turin.

Michael F. Moore is the translator of the novels *Three Horses* and *God's Mountain* by Erri De Luca, *The Silence of the Body* by Guido Ceronetti, the poetry of Alfredo Giuliani, and essays by Pier Paolo Pasolini. He is currently working on a new translation of the classic nineteenth-century novel *The Betrothed* by Alessandro Manzoni.

pushing past the night

pushing
past
the
night

coming to terms with italy's terrorist past

mario calabresi

translated by michael f. moore
with an introduction by roger cohen

other press ⦚ new york

© 2007 Arnoldo Mondadori Editore SpA

Originally published in Italian as *Spingendo la notte più in là. Storia della mia famiglia e di altre vittime del terrorismo*

Translation copyright © 2009 Michael F. Moore

Excerpt from *Mio marito, il commissario Calabresi: Il diario segreto della moglie, dopo 17 anni di silenzio* by Gemma Capra © 1990 San Paolo Edizioni appears with the permission of Gemma Capra

Production Editor: Yvonne E. Cárdenas
Book design: Simon M. Sullivan
This book was set in 11 pt Bembo Book by Alpha Design & Composition of Pittsfield, NH.

10 9 8 7 6 5 4 3 2 1

LIBRARY OF CONGRESS CATALOGING-IN-PUBLICATION DATA

Calabresi, Mario, 1970–
   [Spingendo la notte più in là. English]
   Pushing past the night : coming to terms with Italy's terrorist past / by Mario Calabresi ; translated by Michael F. Moore.
      p. cm.
   Includes index.
   ISBN 978-1-59051-300-2 (pbk. original : alk. paper) — ISBN 978-1-59051-378-1 (e-book)   1. Calabresi, Luigi, 1937–1972—Assassination.   2. Police chiefs—Italy—Milan—Biography.
3. Murder—Italy—History—Case studies.   4. Domestic terrorism—Italy—History—20th century.   5. Calabresi, Mario, 1970– —Family.   6. Terrorism victims' families—Italy—Milan.   7. Milan (Italy)—Biography.   8. Domestic terrorism—Italy—History—20th century.   9. Political violence—Italy—History—20th century.   10. Italy—Politics and government—1945–1976.   I. Title.
   HV8215.M54C3513 2009
   323.3250945—dc22

                                                  2009023471

To Caterina

contents

introduction

by roger cohen

When I was a correspondent in Rome in the 1980s, I was struck
by the recurring headlines in the major papers, which often gave
an impression of déjà vu. The subjects varied, from the latest
political twists to the laws governing rent control, but they provoked the same uneasy feeling that nothing had changed or
moved. One of the most troubling repetitions concerned "Piazza
Fontana." More than a dozen years before I came to live in the
Italian capital, a bomb had exploded in Milan's Piazza Fontana,
killing sixteen people and ushering in the so-called Years of
Lead, a long season of political violence that shook the state to
its foundations. The stories I read under those reappearing
headlines concerned the endless legal back-and-forth over the
Milan bombing—the trials and appeals and retrials—that seemed
to me to make nonsense of the law. Justice delayed is justice
denied. I shook my head and occasionally wondered how I
might write my way through the thicket of charges and coun-
tercharges to shed some light. For, as Mario Calabresi demonstrates in this brilliant book, there were real people and real

pain behind those numbing accounts of judicial peregrinations and paralysis.

Pushing Past the Night is a work of literature. It represents one of those moments when a journalist, often condemned to deal in the ephemeral, combines professional skill with deeply felt personal experience to create a testimony of timeless power. It is a disorienting book, spare and unforgiving, shifting back and forth in time to convey Calabresi's giddying struggle to come to terms with his subject: the murder of his father and the long indifference, or inadequacy, of the Italian state before this crime that shattered his infancy and skewed his life. Seldom have I seen the personal and universal interwoven to such effect, at once disturbing and uplifting. When I lived in Rome, I used to smile to myself, seeing all the stopped clocks dotted around the city. They were endearing in their way, all those useless clock faces seemingly proclaiming the indifference of Italians to time and punctuality. But they also formed their own little monument to inefficiency, inattention, and waste. Time does matter, and it matters most when life and death and justice are the issues at hand.

Piazza Fontana led, by a strange detour, to the door of the Calabresi family home in Milan. An anarchist named Giuseppe Pinelli was detained as a suspect in the bombing and, while in the office of Inspector Luigi Calabresi, the father of the author, he fell through a window to his death. The police inspector himself was not in his office at the time. A painstaking inquest determined that Pinelli, disoriented and exhausted, had fallen by accident over a window railing that was only ninety centimeters high. But these facts proved irrelevant in the hysterical climate of the time. Inspector Calabresi was branded as a CIA agent and "Inspector Murder." The newspaper of the extreme leftist group Lotta Continua bayed for his blood. A weak state—and the state in Italy is chronically weak—did little for its dedicated servant. And, on May 17, 1972, in a death foretold, this thirty-four-year-old police officer was gunned down outside his house by militants convinced they had revolutionary justice on their exalted side. So began the prosaic agony of the Calabresi family.

The author was two years old when the killing occurred. Locked in his mind is the image of his grief-stricken, pregnant mother upon confronting the neighbor who has come to impart the news of the murder. "My memory begins with her cry of despair," Calabresi writes. "He tried to speak with her, but she kept running away, walking from room to room while I clung to her skirt. Frozen in my memory is the image of the two of us in black-and-white, circling for a long, long time. I was worried that he wanted to hurt her, but I didn't know how to defend her. Finally, she stood still, he spoke with her, she wept, and I hugged her legs, feeling lost." It is the achievement of this book to convey the long personal journey of that circling, leg-clutching child to understanding and closure, while at the same time illuminating the recent history of Italy and the national failure to come to terms with the Years of Lead.

Calabresi, now the editor in chief of the Turin daily *La Stampa*, writes in a spirit of reconciliation. His book is an invitation to the Italy of the left and right to come to terms with each other and with painful history. But he is unsparing about what he calls a "romantic idea of terrorism" and about the discrepancy of treatment between the killers and the killed. It took sixteen years to identify the murderers of his father and another dozen years for the various iterations of their trials and appeals. It took until 2004 for an Italian president, Carlo Azeglio Ciampi, to give a medal of valor to the slain police inspector's widow and say these four words: "We have rediscovered memory."

For decades, attempts to honor Inspector Calabresi had to be somehow offset or balanced—and in effect undermined—by tributes to Pinelli. Meanwhile, the militants of the Red Brigades, Prima Linea, and other terrorist groups—their sentences served or commuted, their acts pardoned or indulged—reemerged as politicians and commentators, engaging in public life without public shame. As Mariella Magi Dionisi, whose police officer husband Fausto Dionisi was gunned down by militants on January 20, 1978, tells the author: "The truth is that they gave us a life sentence. They have a second chance at life while we, and the persons whose lives they took, have had this possibility taken away from us forever. I was a young woman and my life was stolen from me." As she speaks, in 2006, Sergio D'Elia, a man who was among those convicted of her husband's murder, has just been appointed secretary to the speaker of the Chamber of Deputies.

One of this book's many strengths is the way it reaches beyond the Calabresi family itself to show the extent of silent suffering from the Years of Lead. Calabresi writes that the Italian state has suffered from a kind of "emotional illiteracy." How else to describe the compensatory offer, for "a daughter of a victim of terrorism," of a job as a Naples street sweeper? Yet this is precisely what is proposed to Antonia Custra, a young woman whose father, a policeman, has been brutally murdered in Milan. How else to view the state's acquiescence to, or failure to control, sex in the defendants' cage at the trial of Red Brigade terrorists charged with the 1981 killing of Dr. Luigi Marangoni, the director of the Milan Polyclinic?

The author's point is one fundamental to the journalist's canon: facts matter. Reconciliation is important, and possible, but cannot be based on an unbalanced accounting of Italy's years of terrorism. His book fills an important lacuna. As Calabresi writes, "Italy has never engaged in a complete reckoning." But this work helps. It amounts to a firm admonishment to the press and a left-leaning intelligentsia that irresponsibility can lead to bloodshed. In the years between Pinelli's fall and Inspector Calabresi's murder, myth masquerading as fact inhabited the Italian media. Almost nobody bothered to check the facts. Hundreds of intellectuals signed a petition that appeared in 1971 in the weekly magazine *L'espresso*. It called the police officer "Inspector Torture," the man "responsible for the demise of Pinelli." Few of the signatories ever apologized, but one or two did, and that's important, even if such belated assumptions of responsibility cannot bring back a life.

Calabresi writes, "Justice is the duty of the state," but the Italian state has too often proved "an empty shell." If a shallow, too pliable, partisan, or venal press does not hold the state accountable, the way is open for the worst to happen. Even as it transcends journalism, this book is a reminder of the fundamentals of the journalistic craft and of the centrality of a vigorous press to any liberal democracy.

But in the end, beyond politics, *Pushing Past the Night* is a personal story, riveting in its directness. Calabresi reveals how the anger of his younger brother, Luigi, is rawest and hardest to tame. Luigi was not yet born when his father was killed, and he tells his brother: "The difference between us is that he never held me in his arms." Calabresi writes, "Mama remembers the leap she felt in her belly when she received the news of the murder and she understands him. 'When I see his anger, I feel exactly what I felt that day.'" Phrases like that "leap" in the belly, where unborn Luigi is curled, twist the insides of any sentient reader and usher in a new understanding of the Years of Lead.

Anger, however, is not what prevails in these pages. Indeed, it is perhaps in the author's victory over anger that this book is most unforgettable. Calabresi had to write his way through his disoriented rage and his pain to produce this testimony; in so doing he reconciles himself with his past and Italy with a neglected facet of its story.

If he succeeds, he clearly owes an enormous amount to his mother, simply "Mama" in these pages. Mama is a remarkable figure, choosing love over vengeance, engagement over despair, faith over depression, and generosity over spite. Left with three young boys, she raises them to vindicate, through their spirit and openness, their lost father's life. For Inspector Calabresi was an open man. He reached out in life, across a political chasm, to Pinelli, the better to understand him. Pinelli once gave him a book as a gift. Mama urges Calabresi to respect Pinelli and the loss felt by Pinelli's children. When Ovidio Bompressi is finally convicted of Inspector Calabresi's murder, Mama is distressed at the thought of Bompressi's daughter losing a father. Her enduring lesson to her sons is one of compassion, honesty, and understanding.

One day, beneath the summit of Mont Blanc, Calabresi grasps all his family's lessons and comes to terms with the loss of his father. "I had to carry him into the world with me, not humiliate him with arguments and rage, if I did not want to betray him," he writes. "I had to place my bets on love and life." In grasping this lesson at the end of an arduous and superbly rendered personal odyssey, Calabresi has also given a lesson in openness and truth to his country, and said something universal about the human condition.

translator's note

On December 12, 1969, a bomb exploded at the Banca Nazionale dell'Agricoltura in Piazza Fontana, in the center of Milan, taking the lives of sixteen people and wounding eighty-eight others. This massacre inaugurated more than a decade of political violence in Italy that came to be known as the *Anni di Piombo*, the Years of Lead. Although the bombing was ultimately proven to be the work of neofascists, the police investigation focused initially on the anarchists, several of whom were brought in for questioning at police headquarters. One of them was Giuseppe Pinelli. After being held for three days, he fell to his death from an office on the fourth floor. That office belonged to Luigi Calabresi, the father of the author of this memoir.

A few months earlier, a militant political movement had formed on the far left. Lotta Continua started out as a coalition of factory workers and students offering a more radical alternative to the more centrist Italian Communist Party. Through its newspaper of the same name, it seized on the general outrage over the Piazza Fontana bombing as a rallying cry for public demonstrations against the government, which it called the true perpetrator of the massacre. The Lotta Continua paper also launched a virulent press campaign against Luigi Calabresi, whom it blamed for the death of Pinelli. Other major periodicals soon followed suit. A judicial inquiry and two court sentences established his innocence, but far too late. On May 17, 1972, Inspector Calabresi was gunned down in front of his home. The comment in *Lotta Continua* the next day was, "This act fulfills the desire of the oppressed for justice."

These are just two events in the murderous cross fire between extreme factions on both sides of the political spectrum that took place during the Years of Lead. On the right, neofascist extremists exploded bombs in public places, including Piazza Fontana in Milan, Piazza della Loggia in Brescia (May 28, 1974), and the central train station in Bologna (August 2, 1980). On the far left, terrorist cells such as the Red Brigades and Prima Linea carried out a series of targeted assassinations, generally of police officers, prosecutors, judges, and journalists. Their violence culminated in the Red Brigades' kidnap and murder of former prime minister Aldo Moro in the spring of 1978. Both the left- and the right-wing terrorists claimed, paradoxically, that their actions were aimed at destabilizing the Italian government and society and ushering in a government that more closely reflected their own political views.

The climate of terror was further aggravated by the Sicilian Mafia, particularly in the 1980s and '90s. Despite obvious differences in its politics and motivations, the Mafia used tactics not unlike those of the extremists in retaliating against government investigations that threatened to erode its power. In 1982, for example, it assassinated General Carlo Alberto Dalla Chiesa, the government-appointed anti-Mafia czar, and, in 1992, two of the most successful anti-Mafia prosecutors (who had earlier scored major victories against the Red Brigades), Giovanni Falcone and Paolo Borsellino. Ultimately, the same judicial strategy was deployed to help defeat both red terrorism and the Sicilian Mafia: the offer of reduced sentences to turncoat witnesses, known in Italian as the *pentiti* or penitents.

Despite countless investigations, legal proceedings, and publications regarding the crimes committed during the Years of Lead, the Italian public remains largely skeptical of "official" explanations and anxious for a more complete reckoning. Their hunger for truth has been exacerbated by the early release of many convicted terrorists and the election or appointment to public office of some of them. Some former terrorists took refuge in France, where they benefited from the so-called Mitterand doctrine (repealed in 2002), the country's policy not to extradite them to Italy. More troublesome, perhaps, is the romantic aura that still surrounds the Red Brigades, which may have inspired copycat crimes such as the assassination of two leading labor experts, Massimo D'Antona (in 1999) and Marco Biagi (in 2002) by the self-styled "New" Red Brigades.

The case of the Luigi Calabresi homicide demonstrates how the crimes of the 1970s continue to play out even today. After the investigation into the murder went cold, there were no new leads until 1988—sixteen years later—when the driver of the getaway car, Leonardo Marino, turned himself in. On the basis of his testimony, three accomplices, Adriano Sofri, Giorgio Pietrostefani, and Ovidio Bompressi—all former members of Lotta Continua—were arrested for the crime. The first trial concluded on May 2, 1990, with the conviction of all four men, and a reduced sentence for Marino. All in all there would be seven trials over a thirteen-year period, variously nullifying and reinstating the original verdict. The final sentence was handed down on January 2, 1997, but seven more attempts would be made to reopen the case, ending in 2000.

Throughout the years the most famous of the three, Adriano Sofri, has maintained his innocence, with the support of noted journalists and intellectuals who complain that there has been a miscarriage of justice. Yet until recently, when he admitted what he termed his "moral co-responsibility" for the Calabresi murder, he has been unwilling to counter the accusations against him with his own version of the facts. Many other noted former terrorists likewise tease the public with the promise of the "true story" of those years, but are never willing to acknowledge the irreparable harm they have caused to the hundreds of Italians whose lives were ended or tragically altered by their actions.

In translating this book, I have adapted it for readers unfamiliar with the historical background or the intricacies of the Italian political and justice systems. The original edition assumes knowledge of the facts and the personalities that very few non-Italians command; it cites movements, national newspapers, and public figures that resonate powerfully with Italians, thus erasing the need to indicate their political orientation or ideological relationship to the events in question. Since a more literal translation would have made parts of this story inaccessible to the American reader, I decided, in consultation with the author and the editor, to insert brief explanations, and often a simple adjective, to make popular or political associations more explicit. At the same time, I have eliminated the names of people who relate only peripherally to the main narrative, such as national media figures and local politicians. To provide a frame of reference for the book as a whole, I have written this translator's note; although it might seem to exceed the boundaries of a more narrow and technical concept of translation, it attempts to express the broader cross-cultural vocation that good translation seeks to fulfill.

The political landscape traveled in this book is particularly complex, since the events related are considered within two very different and very dynamic time frames, the 1970s and today. At the time of Luigi Calabresi's murder, there was a multitude of parties on the left, the largest being the Italian Communist Party and the Socialists, as well as several more militant "extra-parliamentary" formations, including Lotta Continua and Autonomia Operaia. On the right was the centrist Christian Democrat Party, which governed Italy without interruption for almost fifty years. After a series of corruption scandals in the early 1990s, the old system collapsed. The Italian Communist Party split into the centrist Democratic Party of the Left and the hard-line Communist Refoundation. On the right, the Christian Democrats were disbanded, the separatist Northern League emerged as a major contender, and the Italian Social Movement—the heir to the Fascist Party—was reborn as the National Alliance. The biggest conservative player today, however, is Forza Italia, the party of Silvio Berlusconi.

The Italian legal system is best described as byzantine. Trials can drag on for years, and an initial conviction is often followed automatically by a second trial on appeal, and a third trial to confirm the legitimacy of a sentence, which could overturn the previous verdicts, and order that the whole process be started over again. Rather than guarantee the validity of a verdict, these multiple steps and the inconsistency of their outcomes tends to sow confusion and create fertile terrain for often outlandish conspiracy theories, a trend the Italians describe as *dietrologia* (literally, behind-ology, based on the sense there is always a dark truth hiding "behind" the official version).

Lost in this quest for justice is the human cost of terrorist crimes. This book casts a much-needed light on the lives that have been forgotten in the battles over historical truth. Rather than devote his memoir exclusively to his own family, Mario Calabresi also gives voice to many other victims of terrorist violence. This is not a manifesto or a political pamphlet. It is simply an attempt to disentangle the stories of the families from the warring ideologies that so irrevocably determined their fate.

pushing past the night

the premonition

THERE WAS NOTHING NORMAL about the day he was killed. But no day had been normal for quite a while, so his murder wasn't entirely unexpected. Premonitions, panic attacks, anxiety, and even tears had become my parents' constant companions. No one could say exactly when it started. Or maybe one could. Perhaps it was the evening that my father came home, shaken, and announced, "Gemma, Pinelli is dead." Or the day that graffiti calling my father *Commissario Assassino*—Inspector Murder— started to appear on walls throughout the city. Or the morning that the ferocious press campaign began, filled with violence, sarcasm, threats, promises, and taunts. And then there were the political cartoons. Not long after I was born, the newspaper of the militant left, *Lotta Continua*, printed one in which my father is holding me in his arms, intent on teaching me how to use a toy guillotine to decapitate a doll representing an anarchist.

The details that I have collected over the years and filed away in my memory have transformed an ordinary day into a fateful one. Foretold. Almost expected.

You could say that my parents had been preparing for the tragedy to explode for some time. Unconsciously. Almost irrationally. When I try to imagine those moments today, those days of wavering between composure and despair, I find it hard to breathe. I struggle to understand how we were able to survive. First together, as a family. And then my mother, by herself.

Now I'm finally writing, but for years, as far back as I can remember, I've been filing away memories, conversations, secrets.

With my mother, you can only talk about that period in small doses. Her pain is reawakened so quickly that you can only make brief incursions into the past. If you linger in the early 1970s for too long, you risk reopening old wounds. So it's best to restrain your curiosity.

With my maternal grandmother, Maria Tessa Capra, you can talk for hours. She was born two years before the Russian Revolution and lived through two world wars, the bombing of her house, and a husband imprisoned in Germany. She was widowed and lost one of her seven children, but she never stopped fighting. But the only way you can talk to her, to be honest, is for hours: if you sit down on her sofa or on one of her kitchen chairs and ask a question about the past, you had better have plenty of time. Anything less would be meaningless. She likes to remember, loves to remember, even if it does sometimes cause her pain. From her I learned the magical and healing value of words and the importance of sharing memories.

With my father's friends, who I used to visit over the years, the best approach was always to ask a few extremely cautious questions. To avoid breaking into closets filled with more skeletons than I could handle.

So with the passage of time, I have placed six memories in a row—six images that are symbolic of my parents' ordeal, of their pain:

Grandfather. My maternal grandfather, Mario Capra, was a manufacturer and vendor of fabrics. One Sunday, after lunch, during the worst of the press campaign, he took my father aside and whispered to him, "Luigi, things here are getting too dangerous. It's time to quit the police force. Let's find you another job: I can get something for you in Rome, so you can leave Milan and its demons behind. You'll make more money, I swear." According to my grandmother, my father interrupted him right then and there, just as my grandfather was trying to win him over with a joke about government salaries. His answer was laconic. "Thank you, you're too kind, but I could never accept. It would mean that I was running away, that I was trying to escape. It would be like admitting I was guilty. I'll stay until the end, looking everyone in the eye." That night my grandfather couldn't sleep. He stayed up late speaking with my grandmother from the bed of their big house near the San Siro soccer stadium. "He has chosen his destiny. There's nothing we can do to save him."

The mail. For my mother, everything became distressingly clear when she noticed that the mailbox was always empty. One day the mail suddenly stopped coming. When she asked the doorman, he replied, "I keep putting it in the box. Ask your husband." When she did, he denied everything, saying that there was simply less mail. He made a few jokes that time has erased and then he changed the subject. My mother became suspicious. One morning, she invented an excuse to leave the house before him. She looked in the mail slot and saw a letter with an address written in Magic Marker. Rather than pick it up, she left it there and waited. When later on she went back out with the stroller, the mailbox was empty. She waited until evening to ask my father, "Was there any mail this morning?" When he said no, she realized what was happening and felt something die inside. Letters had been arriving filled with insults and threats. He hid them from her so that she wouldn't become even more frightened.

Many years later, she would come to appreciate the love behind a gesture that may have permitted them a few more weeks of normality, no matter how limited.

The note. His friends like to tell stories that they have repeated over the years of his confidences, of the letters in which he disclosed his fears, his presentiments. One particular scrap of paper has always moved me: a note scribbled on a piece of newspaper that my mother found in his wallet, showing how inadequate and even naïve his defenses were. It gives the license plate of a car and then reads, "11.3.71. They're following me. Two young guys in a car. Writing down my license plate."

The premonition. One morning, on Corso Vercelli, exactly one week before the murder, while she was holding me with one hand and pushing the stroller carrying my younger brother, Paolo, with the other, Mama looked at her reflection in the pharmacy window and thought, "I'm a widow." First she tried to banish the thought, then couldn't take it anymore and started sobbing in the middle of the street.

The pistol. My father had a police gun, which was normal. A small revolver. He kept it unloaded in a drawer, hidden between some sweaters. One morning, while my mother was straightening up the house, she noticed it was missing. When she asked him why, he answered that he had taken it back to police headquarters, where it would stay. She pressed him for an explanation, but he cut off the discussion, saying, "Gemma, let's forget about it. I don't want to keep it here. And I don't want to carry it with me. And besides"—at this point he brought up an idea that he had also mentioned to his friends, who couldn't believe that he walked around without a gun—"it wouldn't matter anyway: if they shoot me, they'll shoot me from behind. They'll never have the courage to look me in the eye when they shoot. And even if I did have enough time to react, I would never shoot anyone."

The promise. Four or five days before he was killed, probably on Friday, May 12, or Saturday, May 13, 1972, my father took me to my grandparents' house. He was leaving me there to sleep over so that he and my mother could go out to dinner that night. At the door, before he left, he asked my grandmother, "Mama"— which is what he had called her ever since they became close, even if she was his mother-in-law—"promise that if something happens to me . . ." She tried to stop him. She even put her hand over his mouth, but he still managed to tell her, "Please, Maria, promise me that you'll take care of Gemma and the children." All she could do was nod, with a lump in her throat, while he was hurrying away.

You might think that this is only the suffering of one family, six frames from a home movie. But there is an entire film to see, and for years I have made it my mission to watch it from start to finish, in the hopes that I might one day understand. Although the brute violence of the threats was plain for all to see, almost no one seems to have realized the tragic turn that this campaign of hatred would take.

My curiosity to know, to find out what had been said and written about my father, took root when I was fourteen years old. In my first year of high school, I started to skip class to check out the newspapers in the periodicals room of the Sormani Library, a few hundred yards from the courthouse where the trials of my father's murderers would take place. I spent a lot of time there, with an occasional break every few months, at least until the end of my first year of high school. I would get there early in the morning and wait for the main entrance to open so that I would be one of the first to go in. I would rush in with my microfilm requests: to avoid lines and long waits, I often prepared the yellow request slips ahead of time. First I would read through back issues of Italy's top mainstream newspaper, the *Corriere della Sera.* I started with its coverage of the Piazza Fontana massacre, which triggered the series of events leading up to my father's death, and got as far as the day of his murder. It was a solitary and methodical task that left me exhausted, with my eyes aching, but hooked. I immersed myself in another era, completely losing my sense of time. I would erase all thoughts of school, quizzes, homework, and my classmates. It was an all-consuming experience. Sometimes I felt like a bystander, as if I were observing the events from far away and they had nothing to do with me. Other times the anguish would make my mouth dry and my legs numb. Then I would stand up, rewind the microfilm, and move to the next room, the video room, an amazing, fascinating place with an exceptional collection. You would choose a movie, then wait at your chair in front of the video screen for the clerk to load it into the VCR. It was an extraordinary public service, a fitting symbol of a great modern city like Milan. To stay in historical context, or maybe just because I was a prisoner of those years, I would ask for films from the 1970s, by directors like Fellini, Truffaut, and Kubrick. I would always watch alone, always in silence. At the end of every morning, to return to the present, I would take a walk to the Luini bakery, on the other side of the Milan cathedral, the Duomo, where I would order fresh *panzerotti* with tomato and mozzarella: for years they were my lifesaver, the switch that turned my life back on. I would get two and eat them on my way home, on a route that took me past the ancient fortress of the city, the Castello Sforzesco.

As I got deeper into my research, I started to check the magazines, starting with the left-leaning weekly *L'espresso*. Ultimately I got to *Lotta Continua*, which published diatribes written by my father's most virulent critics, some even calling for his murder. It was a jarring experience, to say the least.

Even today when I read what they wrote, even when I try to put things into perspective and acknowledge their sense that the "enemy" state was too opaque, I still can't stomach sentences such as this one, from June 6, 1970: "That American lackey with the broken window will have to answer for his crimes. We know where he lives." Or this article from October 1, 1970, one week before *Lotta Continua* was sued for libel by my father (a lawsuit that quickly backfired and turned into yet another public attack on him): "We've been too nice to Police Inspector Luigi Calabresi. He gets to keep living peacefully, to keep doing his job as a policeman, to keep persecuting our comrades. But he has to learn that everyone knows his face, including the militants who despise him. And the proletariat has issued its sentence: Calabresi is responsible for the murder of Pinelli and he will have to pay for it dearly."

The country was spinning out of control, and one young couple—in early 1970, my mother was twenty-three years old and my father thirty-two—was becoming more and more isolated. One night in a burst of enthusiasm she said, "Let's go out tonight, to someplace hip like Brera or the Navigli, someplace that's alive!" He replied with a bitter truth. "I would love to go to Brera, but I'd have to take along an escort . . ." Those few times that he did get out of work early, my aunt Graziella would rush over to babysit me. My parents used to reserve separate tables at restaurants off the beaten path. Or they would go to the movies, their great passion, taking care to go in only after the show had begun, to avoid recognition. "They were an extraordinary couple who lived in growing isolation from the city." So said Antonio Lanfranchi, a Milanese businessman who knew them in those years. He was the author of one of the few tributes to my father in *Corriere della Sera* that was not official or from the family. On May 18, 1972, he wrote, "Antonio Lanfranchi mourns his friend Luigi Calabresi." This was so unusual that Arnaldo Giuliani, the news chief at *Corriere*, looked him up for an interview. When Lanfranchi told me about this episode one afternoon in September 2005, I thought he was lying or maybe exaggerating. Then I went to check, and sadly, he was telling the unvarnished truth: only four private citizens had published tributes in the newspaper to Luigi Calabresi, the father of two children with a third on the way, killed by two gunshots to the back, the victim of a rabid public lynching.

piazza del popolo

MAY 14, 1977, on Via De Amicis in Milan: a young man in a ski mask, bell-bottom jeans, and boots, his arms outstretched in a shooting position, his hands gripping a pistol. The picture is seen around the world. One week later, Umberto Eco writes in the magazine *L'espresso*, "Remember this image, it will become exemplary of our century." It is the emblem of the clash that set Italy on fire, the symbolic snapshot of 1977, of a generation lost to violence, of a year with 42 assassinations and 2,128 acts of political violence.

Everyone knows this powerful picture. For some it became an icon of the Years of Lead, the period of political violence in Italy that started in the late 1960s and went on into the 1970s and early 1980s. Many see it as representing the ultimate defeat of ideas, of political protest. Others identify it with strength and rebellion. But no one goes below the surface. Because if they did, if they turned the picture around and looked behind it, they would discover a complex and almost unfathomable world. I was one of the many who knew nothing about this story, and I only

came to discover it accidentally, thanks to my mother and a ceremony in Piazza del Popolo.

A Roman dawn in May 2004. Piazza del Popolo is beautiful. The light is warm, the air almost cold. A girl in combat boots with facial piercings sobs helplessly. Instinctively a woman embraces her, holds her close, and tells her, "It's a wonderful thing that they're giving this medal to your father. You should be proud."

The day before, the President of the Republic had fallen and fractured his collarbone. There are concerns that he might not be able to present the medals of valor today. Not even the medals to commemorate the victims of terrorism, the gold medals that have taken an eternity to be conferred. The medals that send your mind back thirty years, that make you relive sudden pains for which you are never prepared, pains that never bother with formalities such as announcing their arrival. They just show up and tear you away from the present. And they drag you down to almost forgotten lands, lands that don't seem to belong in Italy. Lands that have been left untilled and hidden from view.

If you were to go to the trouble of turning the picture around, of trying to look back at Via De Amicis through the eyes of the young men aiming P38 pistols, you would see other young men in uniform. Young southerners standing in the middle of the street. Then you would see a bullet strike a twenty-two-year-old boy from Naples who has just arrived in the city. You would see him crumple and die. The next day, the newspapers carry his picture, the only picture of him on file. His name was Custrà, Sergeant Antonino Custrà.

You would have to keep looking, sift through the files, blow away the dust, and see past the bureaucratic rhetoric that designates the policeman as victim number 14 of the Years of Lead. And then you might see something else, something that might make you feel uncomfortable or ill at ease: you would see a young widow fleeing the city, following the coffin of her husband, taking him home. She is not alone. Her belly is swollen. She is expecting a baby girl who will never know her father. But no one has ever looked that deeply. No one has bothered to take the journey from that day on Via De Amicis to the present decade, to the baby girl who became the girl wearing combat boots.

We are having breakfast. For my mother, it's the second time this morning. She got up at 5:30 a.m. so that she could make it to Piazza del Popolo on time. She did everything in silence, letting us sleep in, and she went out by herself. They were rehearsing for Policemen's Day in Rome. Together with the other widows, daughters and sisters, she walked in front of the honor guard. She stopped at the spot marked on the cobblestones with masking tape. She pretended she was receiving the medal from the hands of the president. She allowed it to be pinned to her chest. Then, to her dismay, she had to remove her jacket and give it to an official, who would not return it until the next morning, the day of the ceremony. A group of seamstresses at the presidential palace had to sew a piece of Velcro onto it for the decoration.

That is when they met, thanks to alphabetical order: Calabresi, Custrà. When my mother turned around, she saw the girl's eyes fill up with tears. It was her turn to pretend to receive the medal. But maybe she had been pretending for too long. She started to sob uncontrollably. "I looked around for a second, then broke protocol and before the eyes of an invisible president, of the deserted tribunal of honor, of the piazza that was not yet awake, I held her close and began to stroke her hair. Her name was Antonia Custrà. Her father was killed not far from yours. Via Cherubini and Via De Amicis are not that far apart. But they are separated by five years, from 1972 to 1977, by which time the city was no longer new to blood on the streets."

Something clicks in my mind. All I can think about is that girl. I want to speak with her. She broke the bureaucratic spell. She brought memory back to life. And what she didn't do would be accomplished the next morning by the President of the Republic, Carlo Azeglio Ciampi, and his wife, Franca. Ciampi was the grandfatherly figure who did more than any of his predecessors to restore trust in the Italian state. Because of the broken collarbone, he would not be able to attend the ceremony in the Piazza. But while the protocol men were busy designating a substitute to pin on the medals, the disappointed women who had gathered for the sunrise rehearsal were informed of a spontaneous decision. Forget about protocol. Two busloads of wives who had lost their husbands, along with children who either could not remember or had only vague memories of their fathers, went directly to the president's residence, the Quirinale Palace.

The president has decided that people are more important than ceremony. He appears with his arm in a silk sling, rather than wearing a tie, and his navy blue blazer is perched on his shoulders. He begins to speak impromptu. The state has never had such a human face. It has never felt so near. Carlo Azeglio Ciampi himself wants to pin the medals on, although he can only use one hand. All the while, his secretary-general shakes his head and dangles his eyeglasses from one ear in his trademark style. What a shame no journalists are present.

It's our turn. My brother Luigi makes it just in time. He takes the airplane from Milan without realizing that the program has been changed. A quick-thinking policeman rushes him to the Quirinale from the airport. He's getting out of the car when we are already at the gate. Paolo and I tease him, telling him the ceremony was very nice but it's over now . . . teasing is how we always used to exorcise the tensions, powerful emotions, and stifling bureaucracy of state ceremonies. When we were children, we used to invent games before official ceremonies. On Policemen's Day we would try to guess how many agents in the honor guard would faint in the next three hours. It was our way of surviving. A game, a joke we played before the hearings, the trials, the commemorations at police headquarters, where the bronze bust of Papà wore an expression that was too tense and severe. Before going into the Quirinale we joked that we would break protocol and say all sorts of outrageous things. It was also our way of holding Mama back from the abyss. When her eyes began to glaze over, to become distant, one of us would try to make her laugh, to return her to the present.

But this time it's Ciampi who surprises us, prompted by his wife, Franca, who is the first to break protocol. "My dear ladies, my husband is here for you. He cared too much about this ceremony, despite his fracture. He got hurt because he rushes around even when he shouldn't!"

The president jokes, smiles, becomes emotional. When our turn comes he asks us to speak, then he becomes serious, reaches out his hand and caresses my mother's face, and says to her the words that she has been waiting a lifetime to hear. Words that she had thought would never come. "We have rediscovered memory . . . It is an honor for me to give you this medal, even if it has taken far too long." I have never seen her more serene.

After us comes Antonia Custrà. Today she isn't wearing combat boots. She has surrendered to protocol, but not for long. (As soon as she leaves the Quirinale she will put her jean jacket back on.) Accompanied by her mother, she gets emotional again. Ciampi can hardly believe their story. His wife covers her mouth when Antonia relates that she was born after her father's murder.

I remain behind to speak with her. I get her telephone number. At least once every month I think of visiting her. Then I am paralyzed by anxiety and I postpone it.

We leave Piazza del Popolo and Mama seems young again. She smiles and is at peace. We walk down Via del Babuino and she doesn't want to remove the medal from her blazer. She pats it as if she were a little girl with a new toy. Paolo teases her. "Mama, you look like one of those Soviet veterans who go to Red Square wearing all their medals." She laughs and gets back at him with a retort of her own: "I don't care. Maybe I'm a bit of a veteran myself . . ." It's a special day, so she invites us to have an aperitif in Piazza di Spagna. I still have the bill. We three children decide to live it up: one negroni, one bloody Mary, and one martini at lunchtime. She refuses to follow our lead, preferring a fruit-flavored soft drink. The bill comes to fifty euros even. "Don't let it go to your heads, children. This is an exception. Medals only come once in a lifetime."

I would never have believed that a medal could mean so much. I had always thought decorations were too bureaucratic, a cold stiff ritual. Now instead I can see that the award helped my mother and my siblings to turn a page, and gave them serenity, lightness, feeling.

We go to the Presidente restaurant, right below the Quirinale, and have our lunch al fresco. We are joined by my old colleague Angelo Rinaldi, with whom I used to talk late into the night after we had put the newspaper to bed. He appears with a beautiful bouquet of white flowers. Mama will never forget the morning of May 14, 2004.

a photograph

THE MEETING I HAVE POSTPONED for far too long takes place in Naples on a Sunday in January. My mind is made up. I have traveled five hundred miles to have pizza with Antonia Custrà. I took the plane from New York the night before, but first I stopped over in Milan, at the Palazzo di Giustizia, to pick up a folder of long-forgotten photographs. In it I discover the story of a group of youths who had never picked up a gun before that day; of the Neapolitan youth they killed; of the photograph that fifteen years later would land them all in prison; and of the little girl who was orphaned.

In the larger bookstores in Italy, there is always a shelf dedicated to the Years of Lead. Some of them are bigger than others. Almost all the books are written by former terrorists and, despite their many nuances, tell essentially the same side of the story. Invariably they defend their youthful decision to take up arms against the state, in the delusional belief that in Italy the time was ripe for a revolution. There are also books that reconstruct the main terrorist crimes. But there is almost nothing that tells the story of the victims, the people who died, of the lives they led. Recently some room was found on the shelf for a slim, delicate memoir by Agnese Moro, the widow of Aldo Moro, the former prime minister kidnapped and murdered by the Red Brigades in 1978. It practically screams out from the shelf, so different is its voice from the other volumes. Since its publication, it has been joined by one book that collects testimony from the families of the slain or wounded, and another that tells stories from those years originally heard on a television program. But there is still far too little of that other voice.

"The only thing people remember is his name, which they almost always get wrong. Nothing about him, nothing about us. I would be happy if the few times that my father is mentioned— almost always in relation to the famous photo—they could at least get his name right. His first name was Antonio, not Antonino, and our last name is Custra, not Custrà. I've never understood who changed his name and who added the accent, but there it is every time I've seen it for thirty years now." I realize that I have been making the same mistake. Her manner of speaking is remarkable. She's changed. Now her hair is blond, not black. She's very thin, and rather than combat boots she's wearing designer boots.

"My mother was twenty-three years old. They had married in September 1976 and been living in Milan for a few months. She couldn't fit in and she spent most of the day at home cooking or on the phone with her family in Naples. I was conceived during their honeymoon in Germany, where an aunt lived. My father was happy. He was the seventh child, the first boy after six sisters, and he wanted to have lots of children. He didn't become a policeman to escape unemployment, unlike almost everyone else back then. He had graduated from high school and for a couple of years he even studied engineering. They offered him a desk job but he liked being out on the street. He died on May 15 after being in a coma for one day, and I was born on July 1."

Antonia speaks quickly, directly, without trying to soften the impact of the things she is saying. There is no sugarcoating the sharp edges of her story.

"A part of my mother died with my father. She is still with us, but for thirty years she's been a ghost. She's absent, afraid of everything. She never goes out, never buys anything, never takes a trip, never goes to a restaurant. She returned to Naples with my father's remains immediately after he was murdered. She went to live in San Giorgio a Cremano with her mother. Since then there have been three of us: me, her, and my grandmother. For years my grandmother dealt with everything; then she got sick and it became my turn. I'm the man of the house. I do the shopping, buy the clothes, pay the bills. When I was twenty-one, I wanted a little independence, a job that would get me out of the house.

"I was registered with the state as the daughter of a victim of terrorism. They summoned me to Naples city hall for a job. I had to take a test. I was majoring in sociology at the university and I had studied classical Latin and Greek in high school. I was happy that the state remembered me, and curious to see what kind of a job I was being offered. I arrived at the Palazzo San Giacomo for the interview. They showed me to a lobby and made me wait there. I couldn't believe how filthy it was. Litter strewn all over the floor, bags of trash in the corners. It was really disgusting. Then a city employee arrived with a broom. He handed it to me and said, 'Show me if you know how to sweep. Then you have to pick up those bags: that way we can see whether you're strong enough.' I was speechless. I remembered my classical studies and I looked at him inquisitively. He knew right away what I was thinking and said, 'There's an opening for a street sweeper. We've decided to allow women to apply, too.' I felt awful. This was all the state had to offer me. But I didn't bat an eye. I took the broom and got the job. I became the first woman street sweeper in Naples. I did it for two years. A group of other girls started around the same time as me. People weren't used to it, and the insults were fast and furious. I swept downtown, in Piazza del Plebiscito, and the guys would tease me, follow me around, and whistle at me, saying, 'Hey, you really know how to ride that pole . . .' I'm proud of what I did and I never hide it. I always say, 'I started out as a street sweeper.' By the end, everyone knew me. I was meticulous. I cleaned as if it were my own house. I used to personalize my blue uniform. Christmastime I would wear red and hang ornaments on my cart and around my bucket. Then I filled in an application for the Ministry of the Interior and got an office job with the railway police. The first person to take an interest in me was Gianni De Gennaro, the national police chief. I met him on the morning of the medal ceremony. He asked me how I was doing. 'Not too well,' I said. 'I work in a dark, gloomy office that handles health claims. To be honest, I feel like I'm suffocating.' He smiled at me, nothing more, and six months later they transferred me to the Interregional Office of the Ministry. I know that I have him to thank for it."

She promised to take me out for pizza, but first she wants to take a walk along the Caracciolo seafront, and then to go a little further. We enter the Borgo Marinari neighborhood. She stops, looks at me, and says, "My mother doesn't like to talk about my father. She suffers a great deal, so I don't ask. I didn't follow the trials because I was too little and later I was afraid they would be too painful. For years I've been trying to avoid facing the facts. So I don't know anything about what happened that afternoon in Milan. I want you to tell me about it, starting with the killer's name." She catches me off-guard. This is the last thing I was expecting. I start to think I've really put my foot in it, that maybe I have no right, but the silence between us grows heavy and I can't hold back now.

"The boy that pulled the trigger is named Mario Ferrandi, from Milan. He was twenty-one years old at the time."

She interrupts me right away. "Is he still in jail?"

"No, but I don't know where he lives. I only know that he used to work for a big drug rehabilitation center in Bologna."

She's pensive, chews her lips. We walk for a little while, then I start to tell her what I found in the 236 pages that the investigating magistrate, Guido Salvini, wrote about Ferrandi and twenty-four other defendants in his sentence of September 15, 1990. I try to make her see that the judiciary did an excellent job in uncovering every detail of her father's death, that at least one of the government's bodies had done its duty.

There were two trials. At the first, which ended in 1982, three minors—none of whom was directly responsible for the death of Antonio Custra—were convicted. They were three high school students who had participated actively in the riot. One of them, Walter Grecchi, was sentenced to fourteen years for aiding and abetting a homicide, but objectively speaking his crime was to have thrown a Molotov cocktail. He served three and a half years. While awaiting trial on appeal, he fled to France, where he still lives. His name is on the list of people wanted for extradition that the Italian Ministry of Justice has submitted to the French government on two different occasions. His mother begged for him to be pardoned and allowed to return to Italy, but she died without any hope of seeing her dream fulfilled. Antonia remarks, "I remember her writing to us, too. And to think that others who threw Molotovs are in Parliament or serving as government ministers." For a moment, we almost laugh.

I show her the famous picture of a boy in a black ski mask crouching and firing a .22-caliber Beretta.

"Is that Ferrandi?"

"No, it's Giuseppe Memeo. He's not the one who killed your father. Here he's only eighteen. It was the first time he'd held a gun. But in 1979 he shot and killed a jeweler and a secret service agent. The jeweler's teenage son was wounded in the shoot-out, leaving him partially paralyzed and confined to a wheelchair.

"At the moment the picture was taken, the boys were fleeing and your father had already been shot. It's the final scene. They're in front of 59 Via De Amicis, where there's a big copy shop. If you look at the photo carefully, on the opposite side of the street, partly hidden by a tree, you can see another photographer, Antonio Conti. He kept the pictures he took that day hidden inside a book in his bedroom for twelve years. Those pictures were ultimately the key to solving the murder. On October 31, 1989, while the world was changing and the Berlin Wall was about to crumble, Judge Salvini, on a hunch, ordered a search of Conti's home. Thirty negatives from that afternoon were found, providing a trove of additional evidence.

"Using pictures shot by three different photographers, the investigators were able to piece together fifteen sequences that pinpointed each person and his actions. You can see the youths with weapons—one carrying a pistol, another a rifle, a few with Molotovs—advancing toward the third police battalion of the Celere division, which formed a line halfway down the street. Molotovs are thrown, followed by gunshots. Memeo is the first to shoot. The others follow his lead. One guy runs ahead of the pack, staying on the sidewalk to the right and taking cover behind cars. He makes it to within 100–130 feet of the police. He's wearing a light-colored ski mask with a pom-pom and low-cut boots. On the wall behind him is the freshly painted slogan 'Every crime is political.' You can see him shooting even while he's retreating. He is the one who fired the fatal shot. His name is Mario Ferrandi, nicknamed the 'rabbit' because of his buckteeth. He did not realize he was your father's murderer until 1986. The newspapers reported erroneously that Custra had been struck by a 6.35-caliber bullet. Instead it was a 7.65 caliber, so when Ferrandi appeared before the judge, he started babbling that he'd been carrying a 7.65 caliber and had only fired two shots without aiming, so he couldn't be the killer. (His defense attorney was Gaetano Pecorella, who in those days specialized in red extremists. Pecorella later became an attorney for Silvio Berlusconi—as well as one of his Members of Parliament—and for one of the Neo-Fascist defendants in the Piazza Fontana trial.)

"Ferrandi was ultimately incriminated not only by the revolver but also by his boots and the ski mask with the white pom-pom: ten years later everyone still remembered his outfit. In the meantime, he had broken his ties with terrorism. He had still found the time, before then, to kill a drug dealer and carry out his share of kneecappings and bombings. Sad to say, many people would still be alive today if Ferrandi, Memeo, and the other rioters had been arrested immediately. One of them, Marco Barbone, was carrying a sawed-off shotgun and shot a passerby in the face—a news vendor who died from complications of the gunshot wounds. Barbone later murdered the journalist Walter Tobagi, "guilty" of having conducted some of Italy's best investigative reporting into domestic terrorism. Corrado Alunni, another rioter, was also carrying a weapon that day. He became the leader of one of the most violent terrorist groups, Prima Linea, responsible for dozens of political assassinations. Prima Linea was actually born that afternoon on Via De Amicis, in a baptism by fire that no one could extinguish.

The story behind the famous photo is shocking. There were actually five photographers on the street that day, four men and one woman. Unfortunately, the terrorists were able to track down four of them before the police did. Two of the photographers were at the main entrance to number 59: Paolo Pedrizzetti and Paola Saracini. In the sequence of images that was used at the trial, Memeo, after firing his gun, noticed the photographers to his right and retreated. Pedrizzetti managed to escape, making it through the front door and up the stairs to the top floor of the building. He delivered his roll of film to the newspapers and then to the police. As a result of his actions, he was subject to repeated threats by the terrorists. Saracini, in contrast, was too paralyzed by fear to move. Memeo shoved his pistol in her face and forced her to open her camera to expose the film to sunlight. She fell to her knees while the boy in the black ski mask continued firing at the police. The third photographer, Antonio Conti, captured this scene from the other side of the street. He originally told the police that his roll of film had been "violently yanked" from his camera by the protesters, who had attacked and threatened him. But as it turns out, not only was he a relative of one of Italy's leading militants, he was also considered a sympathizer within terrorist circles, and he hid the photos to protect them. No one cast any doubt on his version of the facts until 1989.

The fourth photographer, Dino Fracchi, was able to save his images of the three high school students fleeing the police with revolvers in their hands. He published them, an action for which he paid dearly. One month later, someone set fire to his Milan studio, destroying it and forcing him to live abroad for a period.

"The fifth photographer was Marco Bini. He was wearing a white raincoat that concealed his Zenith camera, and he was able to take shot after shot in the midst of the battle. A few days later, however, he received death threats and was forced to give up his film rolls."

"I have never been to Via De Amicis or to Milan. I reject that city and I don't have the courage to go there. But is there any indication on the street of what happened?" Antonia asks.

[23]

"Nothing," I reply. I had been there the day before, stopping at the point where the police had lined up. I went to the corner from where the shots had been fired and the doorway where two of the photographers had been standing. The copy shop is still there. It's been renovated and is very nice, but there is no remembrance on the outside wall of what happened there.

"What a shame. Anything that would make people remember would be welcome. There is a middle school named after Papà in Cercola, not far from the house where he was born. It was a happy day when they inaugurated it, seven or eight years ago.

"Maybe I should go to Milan. I should read the transcripts of the trial and finally keep my appointment with sorrow. It might help me to get over, to articulate, the grief weighing down on me. I never read detective stories. I'm also wary of the news. I keep my distance from the newspapers, with all their death and violence. The fact that I never knew exactly what had happened filled me with rage, a rage that has no outlet. My mother did tell me—now I remember—that she had gone to the trial and seen the faces of the boys in the cage. She felt sorry for them. I would have murdered them, in the sense that I would have screamed all my rage in their faces.

"Twice a week I see a psychologist. I go from anorexia to bulimia: I have an emptiness I can't fill that leaves me helpless. I lost both my father and my mother. I have to pay the psychologist myself. The state has never taken any interest in providing this kind of assistance. It's not about the money. It's just that they never thought it was their job to support the widows and orphans economically, psychologically, or emotionally. No one has ever assumed this responsibility."

We go for a bite. She doesn't want pizza, so she orders two salads. I try to speak to her the way my mother always spoke to us: about the future, the importance of living again, the destructive power of grudges that devour everything—love, passion, energy.

She looks at me tenderly and replies, "I know you're right, but I can't help thinking what my life would have been like if I had had a father, if I had had brothers and sisters I could play with and confide in. My parents would have had a lot of kids and my mother wouldn't have been the way she is today. Sometimes I obsess over it so much that I can't take it anymore. I fall apart. I'm not at peace. I am alone with too much anger at what they took away from me and all the things I could have had but did not."

4.

the blue fiat 500

In the spring of 1972, I had just turned two. Our memories don't normally go back that far. They get erased. Some impressions may remain, like a spin on the merry-go-round, fish in an aquarium, a ride on a motorbike, a scolding from your parents, a joke by an uncle.

I have two memories from that period. The first is from Sunday, May 14. It's a vague memory of a wonderful feeling, and the only real, palpable recollection that I have of my father. The second is from the morning of Wednesday, May 17, the day of his murder. It's sharp, detailed, precise.

It's as if I had put all my childhood thoughts in a box, a special place I had created where they could survive intact the oblivion of time and maturity. For years I kept them inside me. To avoid ruining them, I took them out gingerly, in the dark, at night, before falling asleep. Then one day I shared them with my mother, but I was already in high school, and it was not until the trials that I spoke openly about my memories of the day that my father died. At one point, however, I realized that my telling and retelling of this memory was destroying it, like the copy of a film that's been seen too many times: the image deteriorates and whole frames are lost. So I ran for shelter and filed them away in an attempt to save them. But maybe it was already too late, and today they've lost some of the overwhelming force they wielded over me for more than twenty years of my life.

But the first memory has resisted and it reminds me that I am his son.

They shot my father at 9:15 a.m., while he was opening the door of my mother's blue Fiat 500. He had just left the house after going back twice, first to smooth an unruly lock of hair, then to change his tie. He had gone out wearing a pink tie, then came back to take it off and put on a white one. When my mother looked at him quizzically, shaking her head and poking fun at him, he explained, "I like this one better: it's the color of purity." She closed the door without giving his words a second thought. She was waiting for a woman who was scheduled to arrive at any moment. They had never met, but the woman was supposed to start coming twice a week to help her out at home: there was too much work, what with two children and a third on the way. She arrived late, out of breath. "My apologies, signora, but there's pandemonium down on the street: someone shot a police inspector."

In the book that she wrote in 1990, my mother recalls that moment:

We were in the kitchen. Paolo was in the playpen, still wearing his pajamas. Mario was playing with his toys. I sat down, ashen. I felt the three-month-old baby inside me kicking at my stomach. The cleaning woman ran to get a glass of water. "Do you feel all right, signora? What's wrong?" "Did you say they shot an inspector? My husband's an inspector." The woman, whom I never saw before or since—a simple, unassuming woman in her forties—guessed the truth immediately. And she knew exactly what to say. "But, signora, you must have misunderstood. I got off the streetcar in Piazzale Baracca. There was a police barricade. They were chasing some wanted men and there was a shooting. They blocked the traffic and I had to do all of Corso Vercelli on foot. That's why I'm so late."

I said, "Let me call police headquarters and try to reach my husband." I dialed the number and asked for Gigi. "One moment please, I'll connect you with his office," the operator said. A few seconds later, someone picked up. "Is Mr. Calabresi in? This is his wife calling," I said. On the other end, I sensed a kind of hesitation. Then, "He hasn't arrived yet, signora. Don't worry. We'll have him call you as soon as he gets in." They already knew what had happened. At that point the phone went dead. The telephone company had been instructed to disconnect it. I tried dialing the police station a few more times, but the line gave no signs of life.

In contrast to her negative thoughts and premonitions of earlier weeks, my mother now seemed more inclined to deny that anything might have happened. To survive the next few moments, she grasped at flimsy explanations and improbable coincidences, hoping to somehow alter the course of destiny.

Until the doorbell rang. When she went to open it, she found our neighbor, Mr. Franco Federico, a tailor and a friend of my grandfather. In the spirit of true friendship, he had bravely shouldered one of the worst tasks that life can assign to you. "Signor Federico, to what do I owe this pleasure?" my mother asked, forcing herself to smile. But he couldn't speak, and he stood there in silence. In an instant the castle of hope that was still standing, despite everything, came crashing down. She retreated into the house, howling, "No!," trying to flee the truth. My memory begins with her cry of despair. He tried to speak with her, but she kept running away, walking from room to room while I clung to her skirt. Frozen in my memory is the image of the two of us, in black-and-white, circling for a long, long time. I was worried that he wanted to hurt her, but I didn't know how to defend her. Finally she stood still, he spoke with her, she wept, and I hugged her legs, feeling lost.

For years I was afraid of Signor Federico. Whenever he came near me, I would start to cry uncontrollably. Every Christmas he would bring me a nice present, but I would keep my distance, and in the first few years I even refused to open his gifts. Over time we were able to reach a compromise: he would place the package in the middle of my grandparent's living room and then walk away. Slowly, furtively, like a cat getting ready to pounce, I would sneak up to it, grab it, and steal away with it quickly to another room. I would circle it for a while and then open it warily. No one came with me. They would leave me alone, giving me all the time I needed. When Signor Federico was about to go, my grandfather would call out to me. Only then would I peek out from behind the door to say thank you.

The last time I saw him, he still had a white mustache and white hair, very thick and shiny. More than ten years had gone by since our last encounter. He was in a bed at the San Carlo hospital, the same place they had taken my father. He was dying. Although he hadn't seen me since I was a little boy, he recognized me and brightened up as soon as I came into the room. We spoke for a fairly long time and then I stroked his hair. It was still smooth, and he told me, "You have given me the nicest gift I could have ever wished for."

People often make lists of wasted opportunities. I also keep a list of the opportunities that were not wasted. That afternoon figures at the very top of it.

• • •

Signor Federico told her, "Gemma, they shot him. He's in critical condition, and they're doing everything they can to save him." With a broad gesture of her arms, taking in the apartment and everything in it, she uttered words to the effect that nothing made sense anymore. I do not remember voices or colors, only images, not unlike Japanese cartoons, in which everything freezes during key moments, especially during combat or athletic competitions. The image goes from color to black-and-white and zooms in slowly for a detailed close-up. As an adult, I used to watch these cartoons with my little brother, Uber, and I was startled at their resemblance to the way my own memories operate.

Signor Federico had just closed the door behind him when the doorbell rang again. It was the deputy police chief. He looked upset, and he said something like, "He has a gunshot wound in one shoulder. They took him to the hospital. We're taking you there now." Followed by "Are you all right, signora? How are you feeling?" I told him, "I'm pregnant with my third child." He smacked the palm of his hand against his forehead as if to say, "This too?" In the meantime, the children had gotten dressed and gone downstairs. A police car, an Alfa Romeo Giulia, had been driven into the courtyard. Outside the main door, on the street, plainclothes police were stationed around the Fiat so that we wouldn't see the blood when we passed by. Someone shoved me in the backseat of a car next to the children and just then Don Sandro Dellera came running and squeezed in next to us. He was the pastor of San Pietro in Sala, in Piazza Wagner, our neighborhood church, where we had gotten married on May 31, 1969. "Take me to my mother's," I told the driver, "I have to leave the children with her." The Alfa took off, tires squealing. I didn't have enough time to speak with the cleaning woman. On her own initiative, she went ahead and locked the door to our apartment, delivered the keys to the doorwoman, and disappeared from our lives forever, as much of a stranger then as the moment she had arrived.

None of us ever went back to that house. My grandparents packed everything up. Mama would never take another step down that street, where a plaque in his memory would never be placed. She promised that she wouldn't set foot there until the day the city finally made up its mind to remember him.

I did go back, almost secretly, without telling my mother or brothers. I felt guilty about breaking a taboo, but I was going to the house of my favorite classmate, Alessandra. One day in junior high, she asked me if I would walk her home—I already knew where she lived—and I didn't refuse. Thanks to her, I was able to reconcile myself with the place where my father was killed. Every time I studied its details and imagined my father's footsteps, I tried to imagine what he had seen in the last minutes of his life.

After a ride that seemed interminable, the Alfa came to a stop in front of my mother's house, on Viale Caprilli. Waiting for me at the door was my sister Aurora. My mother had gone to the hospital. No one was home. My sister Mirella was in Africa, my father in Australia, one of my brothers in Biellese, the other in Germany. "Aurora, take care of the children, I've got to go," I told her. I could see that she was trying to detain me, to put her arms around me. Then I said to the two policemen, "What are we waiting for?" One of them tried to buy some time by claiming that he didn't know the directions to San Carlo very well. "Well I know them perfectly," I replied. "The hospital is near here. Let's get moving!" More hesitations. The police radio squawked. "We're waiting for them to call us from the hospital," the policeman continued. "They have to tell us which ward he was taken to. Would you mind going upstairs a minute, signora? We'll call you when we're ready." The deputy police chief caught up with us. "Go on inside, signora, your mother will be here in a minute." I let them talk me into it, but I realized they were stalling. So as soon as I went in, I gave Don Sandro a look. "Tell me the truth. Why aren't they taking me there?" With a simple movement of his lips, almost wordlessly, he took hold of my hand and told me, "He's gone." Then I finally collapsed onto the sofa.

They told me that I was on the sofa for an hour, holding Don Sandro's hand. After an hour I came to and my first thought was Mario. Since he was older than Paolo he would figure out what had happened, with all those people around. I picked him up, sat him on my lap, and spoke to him as softly and gently as I could. "Mario, Papà has gone to heaven. You'll never see him again, but he can see us. He's gone to make us a beautiful little house where we are all going to be together one day. And there will be trees, meadows, flowers, wonderful toys, and all the things you like. We can speak with him and he can hear everything we're saying, even now." Mario listened without once interrupting me.

The night before, my father and I had played hide-and-seek, as fate would have it. He had been given one more day with his wife and children. One more dinner, a few more pages from the book he kept on his night table, *Khrushchev Remembers*—he used to read early in the morning before having his coffee—and enough time to choose that white tie over the pink one. Fate prolonged his life by exactly twenty-four hours. Fate in the form of a parking garage. Let me explain. Since he didn't have an assigned spot in the garage downstairs, he always had to park the Fiat on the street at night. There was just enough space on the ramp to the garage to park a small car, and whoever got there first could take it. Though my father always tried, especially because it made him feel safer, he almost never got it, since he came home so late.

But on May 15 he got home early for a change, and he was able to claim the spot on the ramp. And the next morning, he was late leaving the apartment. The combination of these two circumstances gave us the gift of an extra evening of play.

We did not discover this until many years later, in 1990, during the first trial. Leonardo Marino, the driver of the getaway car who turned state's witness, testified that the murder had initially been planned for May 16. The criminals had staked out a position on the street very early, but after surveying the area a few times they still couldn't find the blue Fiat. The appointed time came and went. They waited for another half hour, until 9:30, and then, figuring that he had probably left at dawn, they decided to try again the next day.

The evidence for this development did not emerge until the day of my mother's testimony. On the witness stand, she described how a few months before the murder she had started to keep a diary of my father's schedule. She wrote it in a small date book, a gift from the Dutch Tourism Board, with "Holland '72" written on the cover. Her reasons for doing it were partly for fun, partly to make a point. She used to claim that my father wasn't getting paid for all the overtime that he did, so she jotted down in the date book at what times he left in the morning and at what times he came back—often in the dead of night. In the courtroom, she was asked to read the date book aloud. When she came to May 15, she understood why. On that date, she had written, "Gigi came home early tonight." It meant that he had found a spot on the garage ramp and the car was in the inner courtyard, where you couldn't see it from the street. On May 16, she had written, "Gigi leaves at 9:30." On the same page, at the bottom, there are a couple of other lines. "Gigi comes home with chocolates and candies and we play hide-and-seek with Mario."

On May 17, there is a single line. On that day he had been more punctual. "Gigi leaves at 9:10."

My only memory of my father is from the last Sunday that we spent together. The Dutch date book also helped me to reconstruct what we had done that day. "May 14. Gigi takes Mario to see the Alpine Soldiers parade. He comes home with pastries, ice cream, and roses." My mother still has a rose from that bouquet. It's dry, but you can still get a sense of its color—pink tinged with red. She keeps it in a box together with the thousands of letters she has received over the years.

The diary that came back to life and played such a significant part in the trial also brought my mother and me to the memory of that day. The first time we had spoken about it was actually two or three years before the first trial, when I was in junior high school. One afternoon in the kitchen, after having kept it to myself for years, I told her, "Mama, I have a memory of Papà Gigi. It's a strong, beautiful sensation, but I can't place it. If I tell you, can you help me?" I told her about a crowd of people, a public square, and a marching band. I was sitting on his shoulders, a little frightened of the crowd and the noise, but incredibly drawn to the big golden horn of a trombone. He asked me if I wanted to touch it, but I was shy and no one was going anywhere near the band. People were lined up and down the street to watch the parade. No one crossed the imaginary line. Except him. He climbed over something and passed the police barriers. I held on to his hair while he gripped my legs: I was afraid. I felt like we were breaking the rules, but he gave me confidence. We approached the band. He had a word with someone, asked something, leaned toward the trombone, and made me touch it, for just a second. We turned back. I was happy. I felt grown-up, strong, proud to be on his shoulders. I felt like we were doing something very brave. I wasn't afraid of the crowd anymore. Everything felt sunny and warm.

I can still feel that sensation today: vivid, sharp, clean. A feeling of calm and fullness that has descended on me often since then. At school. Amid the crowds exiting the soccer stadium. At Rockefeller Center in New York, when people were fleeing after someone found an envelope containing anthrax spores at the NBC studios. On March 11, 2004, when we were putting together a team of reporters to send to Madrid a few minutes after the bombs had exploded on the trains. On the night we put together the special edition marking the beginning of the war in Iraq.

On all these occasions, different though they were, I felt a warm sensation and I thought of him. It is the legacy he has bequeathed to me. He gave me tranquillity in the midst of chaos, a serenity that settles over me when everything around me is accelerating. The faster it gets, the more things inside me slow down, become clearer, simpler. Maybe it was only the Alpine Forces marching band, but it's a memory I've been carrying around inside for almost thirty-five years.

When I finished telling the story, my mother smiled at me, shaking her head. "How can you remember after all these years? . . . And why did you wait so long to tell me? For days and days after, you couldn't stop talking about that trombone and how you'd touched it. It's incredible that you still remember."

graffiti

Saturday afternoon in Rome. A group of youths breaks away from a protest rally. They're wearing bandannas over their faces and carrying cans of spray paint. On a wall in the center of the city, they spray in large letters *Calabresi Assassino*—Calabresi the Murderer.

From their actions, you would never guess that it is November 2006, not 1970. Telephone booths have long disappeared from the streets and young people are listening to iPods. There are pro-Palestinian demonstrations in the streets, and controversial slogans attacking the victims of Nassiriya, the Iraqi city where a truck bomb killed seventeen Italian soldiers in 2003. And not far away from the rally, a new president, Giorgio Napolitano, has been installed in the Quirinale Palace. The elder statesman of the Italian Communist Party until its dissolution in 1991, his appointment to the highest office in Italy—the first former Communist to be so honored—is a rare moment of reconciliation between the right and the left.

• • •

One year earlier, again in the fall. I'm heading to the international photography biennial in Viterbo with my friend and colleague Omero, to see an exhibit by the Iranian photographer Abbas, whose amazing pictures tell the story of the Khomeini revolution. The show is at the Palazzo Calabresi. I joke that I'd forgotten that I owned a palazzo. But we can't find it. People explain that it's on Via Calabresi. "And a street, too," I add. We start laughing but stop the minute we turn the corner. On the street sign, right beneath the name Calabresi, someone has written *Assassino* with a Magic Marker. Omero starts to say how sorry he is. I shrug my shoulders and explain to him that I'm used to it, not to worry. We go on to have a good time at the exhibit.

July 2004. I'm in Genoa. I walk down the alleys that descend from the Ducal Palace to the Porto Vecchio. I'm looking for a bakery that makes chickpea focaccia. A wall covered with posters and leaflets grabs my attention. I stop to read. There are community center initiatives, newspaper articles under the banner "THE COMMUNIST PARTY," a poster of a missing child with an appeal for help, and a weight-loss ad. Then I notice a handbill with a picture of my father. The title: NO MORE LIES! LUIGI CALABRESI WAS A BRUTE. I remove it gingerly, to avoid tearing it. Although it looks like a relic from another era, it turns out to be new. "HE'S THE ONE WHO KILLED PINELLI, THROWING HIM OUT THE WINDOW OF POLICE HEADQUARTERS IN MILAN. TRAINED BY THE CIA, HE WAS ONE OF THE MOST COLD-BLOODED KILLERS IN ITALIAN HISTORY. MURDERING HIM WAS AN ACT OF JUSTICE. WHO CARES WHAT HIS WHINING RELATIVES HAVE TO SAY. EVERYONE KNOWS THAT EVEN KILLERS HAVE FAMILIES." At this point, I almost feel like laughing, but I keep reading. "MAY THERE BE MANY MORE MAY 17THS, AND MAY ALL THE EXECUTIONERS LIKE HIM QUICKLY MEET THE SAME END." I fold it, put it in my pocket, and try to imagine who could have written it, but it's impossible for me to envision the kind of life that could produce such a leaflet.

Freshman year of high school. December 12, 1984, the anniversary of the Piazza Fontana massacre. There is a memorial march that I attend with my classmates. I thought the event was sacrosanct, but no sooner do we enter the Piazza than a small group starts chanting, syllable by syllable, the slogan "*Ca-la-bre-si as-sas-si-no.*" I don't know what to do, where to go. I break away and head toward the cathedral. Thank goodness my schoolmates follow me.

Over the years, I've come to appreciate the effectiveness of a press campaign that began shortly before I was born. The simple, clear slogan coined in the early 1970s has outlived its original purpose and been passed down from decade to decade and generation to generation. It has proven to be as marketable as today's name brands. But this campaign was not designed by a public relations person: it was the brainchild of many thinkers, including some of the most illustrious names in journalism, theater, culture, and activism. Fueled by indignation, their vindictive fury created a monster. Despite the lack of evidence, motive, or any basis in reality, they decided that my father had murdered Giuseppe Pinelli, nicknamed Pino.

I've often asked myself how I would have felt if I had been a journalist back in that period. My response is immediate: I, too, would have been indignant. The top brass of the police had the duty to explain what had happened to Pinelli, without stonewalling or withholding information. He had arrived at police headquarters on his motorbike, been held for questioning for three days, and died shortly after a fall from a window while still in custody. How was this possible? The police should have conducted a careful and thorough investigation. Instead they were vague and uncommunicative. Their secrecy was an insult to the country and it fanned the worst suspicions. The conclusion is inevitable: the police—my father's employer and a governmental agency reporting to the Ministry of the Interior—had failed to do its duty.

This failure led to indignation, outrage, and ultimately a public lynching. Not of the police commissioner, Marcello Guida, who had quickly announced to the press that Pinelli had committed suicide, claiming that he had thereby implicated himself and admitted tacitly to complicity in the Piazza Fontana bombing. Not of Antonino Allegra, the head of the political office, the man responsible for holding Pinelli so long. No, the public outrage was directed at Luigi Calabresi, the youngest member of the political office. A policeman truly worthy of distinction, he believed that the police should focus their efforts on dialogue with the protesters, not repression. He used to visit the home of the publisher and militant Giangiacomo Feltrinelli (who blew himself up accidently while trying to dynamite electric power installations near Milan), argue with the protesters, and walk alongside the marchers.

In a January 28, 1998, hearing of the Parliamentary Committee on Terrorism and Massacres, the former leader of the Radical Party, Marco Pannella, gave the following testimony: "Between Milan and Gorgonzola on a beautiful day—I think it may have been August 11, 1967—I marched in a peace rally for at least forty-five minutes with Calabresi to my left and Pino Pinelli to my right . . . Pinelli criticized me for telling Inspector Calabresi—politely, mind you—that if he, too, would carry a protest sign, then he could continue to march beside me. Otherwise he could not, even though I was happy he was there. Pino Pinelli protested, telling me that Calabresi was a great guy."

Luigi Calabresi's face was also well-known because he had a soft spot for reporters. He always found the time to speak with them, no matter how busy he was, according to Giampaolo Pansa, who had seen him a few days before the murder. They stopped to talk at the bar across the street from police headquarters. Later on he stopped to chat with another reporter closer to home.

But in the heated atmosphere of those years there was no room for truth. What flourished instead was a series of dark myths about a truth serum administered, a karate chop to the victim, a belated phone call to an ambulance, and an "Inspector Window" who threw Pinelli to his death in the courtyard. While all these legends have long been disproved, a surprising number of people still believe them through a combination of ignorance and bad faith. And they have conveniently and deliberately ignored the essential truth, established beyond the shadow of a doubt: namely, that Luigi Calabresi was not in the room when Pinelli fell from the window and died. Five people were there, but not him. He was in another part of the building getting the chief of the political department to sign the police report. Although every scrap of evidence exonerated him, in the public delirium that surrounded the case no one seemed to care. What ensued was "a ferocious lynching in slow motion. A madness that has infected thousands of people"—that is how Pansa described it in *La Repubblica*.

In my heart, I am convinced that only a minority of Italians today still believe that my father could have killed Giuseppe Pinelli. My family understands this from the way people stop us on the street, the admissions that public figures from those years have had the courage to make, the letters and phone calls we receive. When faced by diehards who still insist on long-discredited theories, some people try to downplay them, explaining that there are always fringe elements who cultivate conspiracy theories, who believe that Elvis is alive or that the Twin Towers were destroyed by the United States government. Others have suggested that I should treat it as a joke.

In all frankness, I cannot laugh about it. Perpetuating false accusations is an insult to our intelligence and a disservice to democracy and civic coexistence. I am not talking about the youths that spray-paint graffiti: they don't bother me. I am talking about the intellectuals and politicians of the far left who keep the tensions alive, fomenting hatred and rancor, by skirting the truth and refusing to go on the record with a clear and unequivocal condemnation of the violence of that era.

The bomb at the Banca Nazionale dell'Agricoltura in Piazza Fontana caused sixteen deaths, and it left a trail of blood that includes Pinelli and also my father. But on December 12, 2006, the thirty-seventh anniversary of the massacre, the speaker of the Chamber of Deputies, Fausto Bertinotti, called Pinelli the "seventeenth victim of Piazza Fontana," without addressing the causes of the railwayman's death. While there were no moral equivalencies or insults in his statement, other people were not so discreet. His words were quickly appropriated to put forward the claim that Pinelli, too, had been murdered, recycling the aspersions that had been tossed around for over thirty-seven years. In its December 17, 2006, issue, the left-wing newspaper *Liberazione* proposed that a commemorative stamp be issued for Pinelli. The paper's editor in chief had made this same proposal earlier, in January 2005, when a commemorative stamp was issued for my father, as if one stamp should offset the other. He observed, correctly, that the prosecutor had verified that Calabresi was not in the room when Pinelli died, but he then revived the most absurd hypothesis from the early 1970s: "Pinelli did not commit suicide. And tons of proof was found that first he had been knocked out, perhaps with a karate chop (or perhaps killed by the blow), and then thrown from the window, lifeless, to make it look like suicide."

In January 2007, the provincial government of Milan issued a decision to place a commemorative plaque in memory of Luigi

Calabresi on the thirty-fifth anniversary of his death, which fell on May 17 of that year. Shortly thereafter the mayor of the city of Milan, Letizia Moratti, announced that another plaque would be placed on Via Cherubini, the street where he had been shot. Together these initiatives sought to fill in a void in the collective memory of the city, but they immediately triggered a controversy in which Pinelli was once again brought into the fray.

The education commissioner, a member of the far left, abstained from the vote on the memorial. In his explanation, he touted the party line. "Not to deny the validity of a healing process, but out of respect for the history of the city of Milan and its citizens, we think that a more accurate historic context would be created by granting equal recognition and appreciation to the innocent victim Giuseppe Pinelli." The commissioner from the Green Party voted in favor, invoking the need for a gesture of reconciliation that should, however, be "coupled with the decision to name a school after Pinelli, the innocent man killed after the Piazza Fontana massacre." At that point the provincial leader, from the Democratic Party of the Left (a center-left formation), stated that the left-wing coalition had voted in favor, and that the far left had abstained rather than oppose the measure. He phoned my mother that same evening to convey the decision, and with great honesty he told her, "We succeeded in making an important gesture, thirty-five years after the death of your husband. Unfortunately we had to associate his name once again with that of Pinelli. I'm sorry about this imbroglio. I'm sorry that we always have to create pain. We should stop comparing the two things. For that matter, there is already a plaque for Pinelli. For Calabresi we don't have anything."

There are actually two tablets for Pinelli on the small plot of grass opposite the bank in Piazza Fontana. The first was set there almost thirty years ago by an anarchist group. It says that Pinelli, "an innocent, was murdered on the premises of the police headquarters." The second, bearing the symbols of the city of Milan, was placed in March 2006 by the outgoing mayor, Gabriele Albertini. It states that Pinelli "died tragically." For a few days the anarchists' tablet, with its false allegation of homicide, was removed in favor of the city's tablet. After a chorus of protests against the "revisionist" mayor for attempting to "rewrite history," it was returned to its place, so that today, grotesquely, there are two plaques—leaving suspended, for now, the question of whether our history will be written on the basis of documents, expert testimony, and judicial sentences, or on the basis of Xerox copies of Lotta Continua pamphlets.

the interview

If they want to issue a stamp commemorating the anarchist Pinelli, then why not give everyone the right to a commemoration, no matter how much time has passed? But they're out of their minds if they're using this measure to reintroduce the idea of first-degree murder. It would be like killing Inspector Calabresi for a second time. He was not even in the room at police headquarters from which Pinelli fell.

So began a one-page interview in *Corriere della Sera* on December 18, 2006, with Senator Gerardo D'Ambrosio, one of the magistrates who investigated Piazza Fontana and the death of Pinelli. The lengthy inquest was not completed until after the death of my father, and it established that Pinelli had not been killed, nor had he committed suicide. He had quite simply fallen out of the window after suddenly taking ill. Although it did not appear in time to save my father's life, D'Ambrosio's investigation nevertheless uncovered all the mysteries of that awful night and established that my father had not been in the room when Pinelli fell from the window.

As I read his words, I am filled with emotion: someone has finally found the courage, the will, and the patience to dismantle the theories that had been recycled for decades. The interview was conducted by Dino Martirano, a courageous journalist who lives not far away from me in Rome. I decide to give him a call, and he immediately invites me over for lunch. At his house, he offers me a tape of the full interview. "I hear that you're writing a book. This should definitely come in handy."

I then phone Senator D'Ambrosio and ask if he can give me a minute of his time. We meet outside the Senate, have an espresso at Sant'Eustachio, and then walk toward the Pantheon. I ask his permission to use Martirano's tape. "It wouldn't look right if I, the son of Luigi Calabresi, asked you to give an interview exonerating my father. You might feel obliged to say nice things to me. But with Martirano you felt free to say what you think and if you don't mind, I'd like to use your conversation with him as a document."

He stops for a minute, shrugs his shoulders inside his navy blue loden coat, and says that he doesn't mind. He does have a few things he wants to get off his chest first, however. As he starts walking again, he says in a dry precise voice: "Pinelli wasn't murdered and your father wasn't in the room. Those were times of complete madness."

Staring down at the cobblestones as he goes, he adds, "I still get letters asking me why I acquitted the police. I did it because I was absolutely convinced that no murder had been committed. Lotta Continua did a lot of damage to Italy: first and foremost, it managed to implant in the minds of the left the idea that Pinelli had been murdered and that the trials were a sham. They weren't interested in the truth. All they cared about was the verdict in their heads: guilty as charged. And they blame me that this didn't happen. I still get letters today telling me, 'You went on to become a senator but you never said why you acquitted Pinelli's murderers.' It's unbearable."

I go home and turn on the tape recorder.

I remember that a file was delivered to me with the label "first-degree murder." I refused to do anything until they changed it to the lesser charge of manslaughter. We had to proceed with transparency. We also had to fight the stonewalling and the ridiculous old-school ways that used to prevail at the courthouse and police headquarters. You can't believe the dirty looks I used to get when I appeared at police head-quarters. I would show up with reporters in tow, to assure transparency and truthfulness. The police didn't realize that I was putting together proof and forensics. We investigated high and low, leaving no stone unturned. And as we pro-ceeded, all the "proof" concocted to show that Pinelli had been murdered—the ambulance, the truth serum, the karate chop, the fall—was found to be without foundation. Let me go through them one by one:

The ambulance. An elaborate conspiracy theory has been woven around the call to the ambulance. So without notify-ing anyone, I took the court reporter with me to visit the center where emergency calls used to come in for ambulance services. I asked to see how the system worked. They took me to the control room. There was a giant illuminated map of the city on the wall, with pushpins to indicate where the ambulances were stationed. They showed me where the ambulance for Pinelli had originated and the time it had been called. They took the register and opened it to the fifteenth of December. On that day, it was recorded that at exactly 12:01 a.m., the Piazza Cinque Giornate ambulance had been called. So we did a test to see how long it would take for an ambulance to make it to police headquarters, because according to rumor Pinelli's body had been left on the ground for hours. We were able to determine, instead, that the ambulance had only taken a few minutes. The time of the fall and the time of the call coincided perfectly. There was no conspiracy.

The truth serum. There was a needle mark in Pinelli's arm. Some people claimed that at police headquarters he had been injected with a dose of scopolamine, truth serum, after which Pinelli felt sick, which is why they threw him from the window. I went to the emergency room, where the doctor on duty told me, "Always the same old story! Go check the newspapers. I can remember a photographer coming in and taking pictures." In the *Corriere della Sera* I found the picture of Pinelli with an intravenous needle in his arm. So his bruise was caused by the intravenous therapy that the hospital had administered to save his life. I went to the newspaper's offices, had the negatives of the picture confiscated, printed them, and put them in the file.

The karate chop. The autopsy mentioned an oval bruise. Claims were made that it had been caused by a karate chop. We conducted an examination after exhuming the body and established that there had been no karate chop. The bruise, as the experts explained, was caused by the amount of time the body had been lying on the marble slab in the morgue.

The fall. There was yet more "proof": the site where the body had fallen. I made a second round of phone calls to the stretcher bearers, the ambulance personnel, the people who were there, and I asked them to indicate the point of impact. We could see that the trajectory coincided exactly with the broken branches on a large bush that had been photographed the day after Pinelli's death. There was also damage to the cornice below the window from which he had fallen.

You can't imagine the dirty looks I got from Police Commissioner Guida when I was conducting these forensic tests at police headquarters. He couldn't believe that a magistrate would dare come to their "inner sanctum" to investigate the police for murder . . .

Only one witness indicated a different point of impact, which was further away. He was a reporter for *Unità*, an elderly man who couldn't muster the courage to get closer to Pinelli. He gave a very general indication. In my ruling, I stated clearly that we had to establish the reliability of the texts, and that the texts indicating the first point were more credible. While I was writing my acquittal, *Panorama*—which was a left-wing magazine in those days—published the opinion of a group of physics professors (still quoted by *Liberazione* today). They wanted to prove that Pinelli's body had not fallen five feet from the wall, as I had argued on the basis of an objective examination, but more than sixteen feet further away. They used the point indicated by the *Unità* reporter, which was eight or nine yards away from the wall, and calculated the average between the points indicated by the eyewitnesses. In my ruling, I was quick to caution them: be careful, my dear physicists, depositions cannot be assessed mathematically; otherwise there would be no need for judges. Proof has to be assessed on the basis of reliability, which can only be obtained through objective studies. Two or three years later, someone knocked on my door. I answered, "Who is it?" From the other side of the door came a voice saying, "I'm a physics professor, one of the ones who signed the opinion. I came to apologize. You taught us all a lesson."

Then we studied the possible variations in the fall and the trajectory, and we conducted some forensic tests in a swimming pool, no less, to establish what had happened. A whole battery of tests were run. In the end, the experts reached the conclusion that the body had been leaning against the railing of the window and then fallen. Let us consider the circumstances: Pinelli had been at headquarters for three days straight, almost without eating or sleeping. He had been brought in on

the night of December 12 and placed in a large room with all
the other people being held. The police soon released the real
perpetrators, the Neo-Fascists, whose views they used to share,
and they subjected Pinelli to an endless interrogation. He probably felt sick, dizzy, and fell from the windowsill, which was
only three feet from the floor. One of the tests we ran particularly irked Police Commissioner Guida: I had a mannequin
made that was the same weight and proportions as Pinelli, to
see where he would have landed if he had been thrown from
the window. From this we deduced that the body could not
have been pushed by others: it had fallen. In short, there was
no proof that Pinelli had been killed. No proof whatsoever.
The most likely hypothesis is that, after the interrogation, he
opened the window for a breath of fresh air, and the hunger,
the exhaustion, and the tension made him feel faint, made him
feel dizzy, and he fell over the railing.

The room. Everyone agreed—including Lieutenant Lograno,
a police officer—that at the moment of Pinelli's fall, Calabresi
was not in the room because he had gone to report to Chief
Allegra. The anarchist Pasquale Valitutti, who was in an adja-
cent room, said that he did not see Inspector Calabresi go by.
I went to ascertain the exact distance between the offices, the
route that Calabresi had taken, and the view that Valitutti might
have had from the point where he was sitting. Valitutti might
not have seen him because in the room where he was being
held there was only one small window that looked out onto
the corridor, and a person would have had to be standing right
in front of it to see someone going by.

And so I issued the decision of acquittal, finding that Inspector
Calabresi had not committed the deed. In the meantime, however, he had been murdered. Then I prosecuted members of
the police for detaining Pinelli at headquarters for so long without an arrest warrant, but they got off following an amnesty.

What can I add? I cleared the anarchists of any responsibility for the Piazza Fontana massacre. I determined—and

history has backed me up on this—that the Fascists did it, and I risked my neck for it. There is no proof that Pinelli was killed and in fact everything argues for a fall caused by a fainting spell. The trial documents are what they are, and I repeat, there is irrefutable proof. After I wrote my sentence they spray-painted on the walls that I was a Fascist. Later on, when I said that the anarchists weren't the ones who planted the bombs, they said I was a Communist. That's Italy for you.

The names of Giuseppe Pinelli and Luigi Calabresi have been linked for almost forty years, a longer period than either was granted to live. They have been pitted against each other in an endless struggle, one of the many that has paralyzed Italy and kept it with its eyes trained resolutely backward. For my family, too, their names are forever joined. As children we were taught that one night Pinelli, like our father, had not gone home to his little girls, and we were quiet when someone said his name, out of respect for the dead. Mama spoke about him sensitively, and said that their destinies were connected, not contradictory. One day she gave me *Spoon River Anthology* by Edgar Lee Masters. While she was handing it to me, she told me that Pinelli had given it to my father one Christmas. He and Papà were not exactly friends and they did ascribe to different political philosophies, but in the house where I grew up, Giuseppe Pinelli was never considered an enemy.

7.

capsized

R HETORIC AND FORM are triumphant at times when all else is collapsing. Imposing funerals, uniformed authorities, the presidential honor guard, the Minister of the Interior paying housecalls, and an indignant political class issuing admonitions and promises: all that's left in their wake are a few small things. The image that comes to mind is a person combing the beach in search of personal effects after a hurricane, bending down to find the things that still belong to him. All that remains is a reality consisting of a slow reconstruction, an exhausting recovery of memories, a journey that for many people turns into a suffering so great that they try to either flee or repress the memory.

Reality is three children sitting on the floor in the evening around a Geloso magnetic tape player listening to the voice of their father reading a fairy tale. We would listen to it in our bedroom, after putting on our pajamas, while Mama stayed in the kitchen. The tape was always breaking, and we fixed it over and over again, until we lost it forever.

Mama with her head on the kitchen table, crying inconsolably.

I remember the afternoons we spent at the cemetery, in Musocco, in the northern suburbs of Milan. We used to follow a ritual: we would buy flowers—we loved white daisies—go fill up the watering can at the fountain, and take turns climbing an eight-rung ladder on wheels to clean the picture of Papà Gigi smiling on his wedding day. We would give him a kiss and then go off to play, leaving Mama by herself. In winter we would race under the porticoes. It was so cold that the water in the fountain would freeze. In summer it was cool and we would hide behind the gravestones in the garden. I once asked my mother why she hadn't wanted him to be buried in the ground, like in the American cemeteries, such as Arlington, where the fallen from many wars are laid to rest beneath the lawn. Her answer was simple. "Because I didn't want him to get caught in the rain. I would find no peace imagining him in the ground on stormy nights."

When we got to the gates, we used to stay silent for a long time. There were small compensations, however. In the fall, there were chestnuts, making everything a little nicer. And there was always our friend who had died as a child. His parents used to place toy cars over his grave. We would play with them and after a while we started to trade: we would bring one from home and in exchange we would take one of his. One day we took two, but at the gates Luigi said, "We can't do it, poor kid." My mother didn't know what we were talking about, but we hurried back to return the car.

Everyday life had its anomalies. Some nights for dinner we would have milk and cookies or scrambled eggs. When we ask her today, "Mama, do you remember? It was so nice to have breakfast twice," she groans, "How dreadful, I feel so embarrassed." She wanted to manage on her own and was too proud to ask for money from her parents, and she confesses that sometimes she could barely make it to the end of the month. But on payday she would buy calves' liver, and for us it was a royal feast.

In the two years following my father's death, we all lived at the home of our grandparents, who showered us with attention and care. Then Mama decided that the time had come for her to manage on her own, taking full responsibility for the three of us. She wanted to hold together through her own strength and resources what remained of the family she had dreamed of having. She rented a house, found a job as an elementary school religion teacher, and made a go of it with all the energy that a twenty-eight-year-old woman can muster. And she succeeded, thanks to our cooperation and a faith in life and God from which she never faltered.

I have to admit that the three of us didn't want her to come to the playground with us. All the other children were accompanied by their fathers. So when we wanted to go we used to wait by Uncle Dino's window. He provided us with a male figure we could look up to, and we thought that if he came along with us to the playground everything would be all right.

Policemen's Day was one festivity that Mama would have preferred to skip. Too much sadness, too much ceremony, too many ritual expressions of solidarity. But we children would insist on going just for the salmon canapés, an absolute luxury. In those days, you couldn't find inexpensive salmon at the supermarket all year round. It used to be available only at Christmastime at our grandparents' house, and serving it to children was considered wasteful. So we were always the first ones at the buffet, and we would empty all the trays before the shocked eyes of the officials and directors. Mama would say nothing. Maybe she thought it was the least the state could do for us. At the Policemen's Day parade we would feel shy and enchanted at the sight of the Padovani girls, who were always dressed up, always perfect.

Their father, Vittorio Padovani, had been killed by terrorist machine-gun fire on December 15, 1976.

For years photographers used to wait for us outside the main door to our house and follow us around. My mother, her hair almost completely gray, would put on a pair of dark sunglasses and quicken her step, pushing the baby carriage with Luigi inside. I trotted behind her and tried kicking them away.

I remember the pressure of feeling different, of not being normal children. We didn't have the right to a first or last name. No, we were "the children of . . . ," a fact that weighed on our every movement, every game, every friendship with schoolmates. Our experience is captured perfectly in the words of Benedetta Tobagi, whose father had been killed seven years after our own, and also in the month of May. In *The Silence of the Innocent*, she writes: "I do not remember my childhood as normal. I had the persistent sense of a double life—one black, one white—of a heavy, suffocating parallel world that I couldn't share with anyone. A child's life is normally measured out in schools: kindergarten, elementary school, middle school. Mine was measured out by the 'Tobagi affair' . . . Ever since I was little, I could remember someone always asking me whether I was related to Walter Tobagi. I remember once at elementary school, I must have been six or seven, I tried to pretend that I lived in a different world, that I still had my father next to me."*

In kindergarten I used to keep my distance from the sandbox. I looked at it from a distance. I didn't want to go near it. It was too dangerous: a place where sadness and humiliation had ambushed me. But it wasn't always like that. On one of the first days of kindergarden, we were all digging in the sandbox with

---

*Giovanni Fasanella and Antonella Grippo, eds. *I silenzi degli innocenti* (Milan: Biblioteca Universale Rizzoli, 2006).

our shovels, in a circle, telling stories, showing off, as children do, with tales about what our fathers made us do at the beach. When it was my turn, I said, after hesitating for a moment, "Mine tells me to make castles." An older boy interrupted me. "That's not true, you don't have a father!" I started to blush, to defend myself, to explain that I did have a father, but it was useless. "My mother told me: they shot your father and he's dead." I left the sandbox in silence and never went back. And when my brothers went there, despite my attempts to dissuade them by claiming that the sand was dirty and filled with worms, I stayed close to the edge, leaning against the wall to make sure that pain—sudden and disguised as a child—would not attack them, too.

Once I started elementary school, I kept to myself. My brothers were still in preschool, so I had no one to look out for. I was alone. During afternoon recess, I didn't go to the playground with the other children, asking instead for permission to stay in the classroom. I always finished my homework before everyone else, went to the small library in the back, and stayed there to read until the school day was over—first comic books, especially *Mickey Mouse*, and then my favorite book, *Robinson Crusoe*.

I felt perfectly comfortable in this bubble of solitude, but it was obviously lined with sadness. The bubble was finally burst in a funny, even clever way by Rosario Carro, nicknamed Iaio, the youngest in a line of brothers who had grown up at the San Siro racetrack, where their father trained horses. One afternoon he stopped me at the door to the classroom and said, "Chief O'Hara, why don't you show us how you play soccer?" He caught me completely off-guard. He knew that there was an inspector in my life, but had turned him into a cartoon character and then turned me into that character. I tagged along after Iaio to play soccer, and he told everyone, "He's the son of a policeman, an inspector . . . Chief O'Hara, as my brothers say. His father is a guy that catches thieves." At the end of the afternoon, I took him aside, near a tree that acted as a goalpost, and asked him, "Do you know that they killed him?" I didn't want to pretend again and risk painful misunderstandings. He replied, "Of course I know. My brothers told me, but we don't have to go around telling everybody." About ten years ago, I was passing by the racetrack—my grandparents still lived nearby. I stopped the car, went in, and asked for the Carro brothers. I was directed to a series of stalls where I could find them. They were all there. Iaio was walking a beautiful bay to the training track, and I went up to him and gave him a big hug.

Then there are the sudden, uncontrollable moments of pain. For the Calabresi children that feeling of being shipwrecked has a name: *Bambi*. Children have loved the Walt Disney film about a white-tailed fawn ever since it came out in 1942, but when we went to see it at the movies, in the mid-1970s, it turned into a catastrophe. We were at the Gloria Cinema, on Corso Vercelli, and we were enjoying the story until the moment that the hunter killed Bambi's mother. My mother started to cry in the middle of the theater. It was so sudden and unexpected that we started crying, too, overwhelmed by our feeling of loss. At the end of the film, we waited for everyone else to leave before getting up. We were embarrassed and for years we never spoke about what had happened.

we have to say good-bye

F RANCESCA MARANGONI looks at me as if to say, *Do you think I'm crazy?* "Of course I've never seen *Bambi*. Nor did I ever take my children to see it." We're seated on a bench in the Guastalla gardens, behind the State University, next to the Milan Polyclinic, where her father was medical director until the day in 1981 that the Red Brigades shot him.

For almost eight years, I've kept a clipping about her from *L'espresso*. In a long article titled "The Forgotten Victims Speak," she describes the sudden pain that sometimes assails her, and the time she broke down in tears in a movie theater. She starts to tell me about it. "I was watching Bertrand Tavernier's *A Sunday in the Country*, a film about an elderly French painter who gathers three generations of his family at his country home near Paris. The classic situations occur: they eat, they argue, they fight. Toward the end, the prodigal daughter arrives, and in the final scene she dances with her elderly father. A farewell dance. She does so knowing that it may be their last moment together . . ." Francesca hesitates and bites her lip. Tears well up in her eyes and she tells me, in a shaky voice, "It made me realize what I would never have. My own father would not be at my wedding and he would never see my children." She is still crying, twenty-six years later, during the lunch break that she has set aside for me.

In a photo that her mother keeps on a table in the living room, the family is pictured during their last summer together, in England, in front of Leeds Castle. Her father is wearing a suede jacket. He's young. Francesca is a pretty sixteen-year-old in red jeans. You can see that they were close.

She refuses to wipe away her tears. "I have two children. One is seven, the other's four, and I've never had the courage to tell them. One day my oldest heard something from his cousin, so he asked me, 'Did Nonno die because of a war?' He thinks there are good guys and bad guys and that in war the good guys always win. It's hard for me to explain to him that there was no war. Only some people who thought they were in a war, who had their minds made up that they were in a war, and one day they started shooting guns. But I don't have the courage to tell him. I can't find the words, so I change the subject. All of this is incredibly painful. Over the years I've had to develop a sense of distance."

Francesca Marangoni works at the Marangoni Center for Transplant Coordination, a pavilion at the Polyclinic named after her father. She, too, is a doctor. "To tell you the truth, I had no vocation for medicine, but it was in the air. Everyone expected me to become a doctor. If I were to be reborn, I would want to be surrounded by books, by paper, not by the dead . . . but I know that he would have been pleased. The hospital was his life. And to think that it was a nurse, a head nurse, who gave his name to the 'hospital column' of the Red Brigades . . ."

A few yards from where we're sitting, they planned out the death of her father, but she doesn't want to discuss former terrorists. She is upset by reports that some of them might become civil servants or serve in Parliament. "At the very least, they should be condemned to public silence: we have nothing to learn from them. If they had to follow a series of steps to be reintegrated or rehabilitated into society, good for them, but that doesn't change anything. No one can bring back what they took away. I don't think they have any more right to rehabilitation than other criminals. But for my own peace of mind, I wanted to look the terrorists in the face: I went to the trial in the courtroom—which looked more like a bunker—at the San Vittore prison. The defendants' cage was like a circle of Dante's *Inferno*. It held the whole Walter Alasia cell, shouting, cursing, turning their backs on us, eating. Once they even started throwing food at us. In the middle of our lawyer's arguments one day, a couple started having sex in front of everyone. The police noticed and all hell broke loose. It almost makes me laugh to think about it today. The judge reprimanded them, demanding respect for the widow. One of their lawyers had the nerve to turn toward my mother and say, 'But the signora is not offended.' She immediately retorted, 'But I am offended!' In other words, they acted like complete jerks.

"Somehow this message did not get through to the public. Throughout the trial, the terrorists were depicted wearing a halo of social commitment, as combatants rather than as losers who had waged an armed struggle to escape their bleak lives, people who were poor in ideas and spirit. The only one who made an impression on me was the cell leader, Vittorio Alfieri. He was always quiet and attentive, and today he is a free man, living in seclusion. After the trial, he wrote us a confidential letter of apology. I don't know what became of the others. I don't think that any of them are still behind bars and frankly I don't care. Luckily the people who murdered my father weren't famous enough to be on television, to give interviews, or to be covered in the newspapers. This was one indignity, at least, that I was spared.

"Once I ran into one of the defendants from the trial at a children's playground. I'd memorized his face. When I saw him again, I froze. I wanted to go up to him and say, 'Look, I know who you are. I saw you in the cage.' That's all. But I regret to say that I never got up the courage to do it.

"I have the impression that society as a whole has only a superficial respect for us and for those who died, under the rubric, 'the family's suffering.' But here at the hospital I find real traces of my father that go beyond the plaques and the commemorations. He is still alive in the memories of the many nurses who studied with him, and in the memories of some of his colleagues. They stop me in the corridors and tell me stories that fill me with emotion, and I feel as if he is near me."

Francesca remembers clearly her father's bitterness when he came under fire at the hospital for testifying at the trial of nurses associated with the militant group Autonomia Operaia who were accused of sabotage. Some militant orderlies had pulled the plug on refrigerators containing blood for transfusions, so it had to be thrown out. They wanted to prove that the system didn't work and had to be brought down. For them the hospital was the symbol of a corrupt society, and Dr. Marangoni a criminal for enabling it to function. By throwing a wrench in the works, they thought they were releasing the social tensions needed to bring about the revolution.

Rather than praising him for his courage in standing up to the saboteurs, some hospital workers passed out leaflets attacking him. "That morning I had a test in classical Greek. I was in my first year of high school at the Liceo Classico Beccaria, and when I got back home he was very upset. He served on the committee that authorized thermal spa treatments, and his opponent had accused him of denying treatments to workers in order to curry favor with the bosses." He had been receiving threats for some time. "I knew, but I didn't think that anything would really happen. But one morning he explained to me that he wouldn't be accompanying me to school anymore. It was best not to take the same route every day. He was afraid they were going to kneecap him. He said, 'Who knows whether I'll still be able to walk or ski?' They chose to go after him also because he was an easy target. If we had lived in the center of town, on a small narrow street where you couldn't loiter or hide, then maybe he would still be alive today."

Instead their apartment was in front of the San Siro stadium, on a spacious street, and Luigi Marangoni was killed while he was driving his car through the gate to the road. His wife, Vanna, was looking out the window to see him off, as she did every morning. "It was my way of trying to protect him," she told me a few hours after my conversation with her daughter. "That day I heard something popping, but it was Carnival, so I thought it was just firecrackers. Then I noticed that his car had stopped and that the exit was blocked by a white Fiat Ritmo waiting by the side of the road. Two people wearing berets and dark glasses jumped into the Fiat and took off. A little further up the road they picked up a third person. My husband's car wasn't moving. It was then that I said to myself, 'It's happened. This time it's really happened.' I ran downstairs in my bathrobe and nightgown. The doorwoman tried to stop me: 'Don't go out. They're shooting.' I told her, 'Don't you understand? They're shooting at my husband!' When I was outside, I didn't see him, so I thought they'd kidnapped him, which gave me some hope. But when I got closer to the car I realized that he was slumped back against the seat. I opened the door, fell to my knees, and put my arms around him. He was covered with broken glass, and was losing a lot of blood from his neck. I placed my hand over his face so he could feel me, to give him some warmth, even though there was nothing left to do. I realized that our life together had just ended and I told him, 'We have to say good-bye.' I closed his eyes before they put him in the ambulance."

· The flyer claiming responsibility for the murder said that Luigi Marangoni was a servant of the state and of the Christian Democrats. His widow, Vanna, speaks in a soft, low voice. "And to think that he'd never even voted Christian Democrat. He was a liberal, a perfectionist, completely dedicated to his job. He had gotten rid of all the riffraff in the hospital morgue, where some of the employees had been cutting deals with funeral parlors. He made even more enemies when he testified at the sabotage trial. Three nurses also testified. They were kneecapped inside the hospital. The terrorists gave him a death sentence. But first they wanted to smear his good name. They passed out a pamphlet claiming that he had been paid off to deny thermal spa treatments for some bank employees. He went home that night and started to cry. It was January 31. He realized the leaflet was a warning sign. He woke me up that night and told me, 'Remember that I'm an honest man and that you have to love me. Please forgive me if I leave you and Francesca alone, but it's not my fault.' That was all he said."

This tiny woman remained silent for a long time, her gaze lost in memories or perhaps in regret for what might have been. Then she added a final thought. "It was a complete waste. It didn't help anyone and I was cheated. They took away a part of my life."

In late May 2005, my mother paid the widow a visit, and they spoke for a long time. Mama was also struck by her quiet tone and heavy sadness. When she left, she called me from her cell phone on her way home. My mother is a person who believes in moving on, in always looking forward, in reconciliation and forgiveness. She is sustained by her strong, fervent faith. But that afternoon, her voice was shaking. She told me, "You see, Mario, I listened to her for a long time. It made me think again of my children, of Papà Gigi, of all the people that we've met over the years who haven't found the strength to go on living, of what the terrorists did to us, of how we were all left alone, and how the parade passed us by. We were too nice about it, too patient."

the chamber of deputies

THERE IS A POINT when the normally mild-mannered, easygoing, civic-minded people who go by the reassuring name "the relatives of the victims" start to grow restive. They rebel, they speak out. Not that anyone notices. In a country that's used to full-throated protests, to people lying down on railroad tracks or occupying the stage at pop music festivals, the relatives' words fly well under the radar. Their protest takes the form of angry letters or threats to return commemorative medals. Respect for the dead prevents them from giving full vent to their feelings, but the pain underlying these small gestures is of terrifying dimensions.

These sudden eruptions never stem from a single provocation. They always come after a series of insults, affronts, slights. I have developed a key to understanding these outbursts through my passion for cataloging. I've learned to predict and sometimes even staunch them, warning government officials that malcontent was growing and would soon erupt, somewhere. Luckily not everyone turns a deaf ear. Some officials have shown that they understand these delicate moments and, in silence, without fanfare, without seeking political gain, have tried to heal the pain.

One such instance was the day in July 2004 when, after years of stalling, Parliament finally approved in committee, by a unanimous vote, new regulations to benefit the victims of terrorism and massacres. Shortly thereafter, however, problems arose with funding the measure. So for many victims, the promised restitution has been a dead letter. Five years have gone by and the law has still not been fully implemented. Exasperation has led some family members to take a step that they would never have contemplated earlier: they decided to file suit against the state.

The malcontent of the families comes from their sense that the state has ignored or abandoned them. Their feelings are easily understood in light of an unfortunate series of events in spring 2006 that combined chance, carelessness, and a remarkable lack of political, historical, and cultural sensitivity. On May 31, a few days after he was sworn in as president of Italy, Giorgio Napolitano issued a pardon to Ovidio Bompressi, the convicted murderer of my father. The decision had actually been made and finalized under the previous president, Carlo Azeglio Ciampi. The only thing that Napolitano did was affix his signature to the document.

The problem is that no one alerted us beforehand. I was on my moped one day when my cell phone rang, not with one call but with two. They were from Luigi Contu, my boss at the ANSA news agency, and Arturo Celletti, the political reporter for the Catholic newspaper *Avvenire*, calling to warn me that the wire services were carrying the story about the pardon. I was flabbergasted. My cell phone fell from my hands and was crushed beneath the wheels of a passing bus. I raced home to phone my mother before reporters called seeking her comments. Luckily she was in the park watching her grandchildren play on the trampoline. When I told her the news, she was beside herself. Not because of the pardon itself, which we had never opposed, but because of the sloppy and off-handed way it was handled. Thanks to confusion and mismanagement, a potential gesture of appeasement had been turned into a slap in the face.

Allow me to explain my position. I don't think that the government should be required to seek the victims' permission before passing laws or deciding whether to grant pardon, parole, early release, or supervised furloughs. Such matters should be carried out in the general interest, which might not necessarily coincide with the interests of the "families of the victims." If the state, the judiciary, the government, or the president thinks that an act is appropriate, necessary, and justified, then the pain of private citizens should obviously not be an impediment. Nor is there any requirement that the families be notified. But there is plain common sense: the sensitivities, kindnesses, and gestures that can ease the pain and help people to accept it. Let us remember that most of the people killed in the Years of Lead worked for the state and paid for their service with their lives. Rather than pay tribute to their sacrifice, the country seems to be suffering from a kind of emotional illiteracy.

My mother's phone started ringing nonstop after the news of the pardon was broadcast. The calls were not from politicians or even journalists, however. They were from people like Carole Tarantelli, the widow of Ezio, a jurist killed by the Red Brigades at La Sapienza University in 1985; Marina Biagi, the widow of Marco, the expert in labor law killed by the New Red Brigades in 2002; representatives of victims' associations; people who had been kneecapped by the Red Brigades, like Maurizio Puddu, or who had lost loved ones in the bombings, like Manlio Milani, whose wife died in the Piazza della Loggia massacre in Brescia. All of them were angry. Some wept with rage. There was also a call from Rosa Calipari, who had lost her husband in Baghdad when he was killed by an American soldier while accompanying the kidnapped journalist Giuliana Sgrena to freedom.

The next day Giorgio Napolitano telephoned—early in the morning, after reading the newspapers, which had drawn attention to the fact that the family had not been notified. He explained that the presidential palace had been convinced that communications were being handled by the Ministry of the Interior. The phone call was long, clear, and direct, and helped to forge a relationship of mutual esteem and respect.

In early June 2006, Sergio D'Elia was appointed secretary to the speaker of the Chamber of Deputies. A newly elected deputy, he had run on the slate of Rosa nel Pugno (Rose in the Fist), a coalition of the Radical and Socialist parties. Before entering the political arena, he founded the human rights organization Hands Off Cain, which advocates the abolition of the death penalty. But in the 1970s he had also been a militant in the armed struggle, as a member of the terrorist group Prima Linea. For his role in the January 20, 1978, murder of Fausto Dionisi—a police officer killed during the attempted escape of a group of terrorists from a Florentine prison—D'Elia was sentenced to thirty years in prison, which was reduced to twenty-five on appeal. After serving twelve years, his sentence was commuted by the Rome Tribunal in 2000. His civil rights were restored, despite the objections of Dionisi's widow and his daughter, Jessica, who was two and a half at the time of her father's death.

They bristled with indignation: how could a former terrorist be seated in Parliament? And promoted to the position of secretary to the speaker of the Chamber of Deputies? Politicians were split over the issue: some rode the wave of political indignation, while others defended the decision with heartless arguments. Once again the debate quickly dispensed with the victims and shifted to the rights of former terrorists: the right to build a new life, to be reinserted into society, to freedom of speech. They had paid for their crimes—this was the most popular expression—and now they had the right to live like other people.

"I took it very badly. This time I was absolutely sick over it: I already had to struggle to digest the fact that he had been elected to Parliament. Then when I found out that the same man who had been convicted as an accessory to the murder of my husband had become the secretary to the speaker of the Chamber of Deputies, I was mortified: this was really impossible." Mariella Magi Dionisi was twenty-two when her husband, Fausto, who was a year older, was killed. Her voice is lively, with a strong Tuscan accent. She is not the type of person who lives withdrawn from the world. She founded Memoria, one of the most active associations representing the victims of terrorism. For years she has been fighting for laws to remember the victims and to grant damages and assistance to their families.

"There are things that are intolerable, that go beyond the pale. I don't question the laws or allowing terrorists to rebuild their lives, but the least I would expect from the terrorists and from the government is respect and some sense of decorum. From the former terrorists, I also expect silence and a refusal to take part in public debates, if for no other reason than to avoid opening old wounds. Because the truth is that they gave us a life sentence. They have a second chance at life while we, and the persons whose lives they took, have had this possibility taken away from us forever. I was a young woman and my life was stolen from me."

She pauses for a minute and then begins to explain her thinking more precisely, to avoid being misunderstood. "I wasn't offended by the fact that Sergio D'Elia was the secretary of Hands Off Cain. Everyone should work for a cause he or she believes in. It's what happened later that shocked me. The debate in the

Chamber, followed by the controversy in the newspapers, was truly indecent. The politicians outdid themselves to defend D'Elia, themselves, their decisions, and their behavior. D'Elia did not utter a single word of remorse. His defenders in the Chamber failed to pronounce even one word of remembrance for the man who had been murdered. I felt so alone after that day. A wave of depression came over me. Thank goodness some people spoke out, particularly in Florence, where the mayor, the speaker of the regional assembly, and representatives of every party expressed their solidarity. I especially appreciated the fact that many town councillors, some from very small towns in 'Red' Tuscany, felt strongly enough about this to vote in favor of a motion asking D'Elia to turn down his appointment."

Mariella Magi Dionisi feels as if she's been condemned to spend her whole life in the shadow of the late 1970s. She finds her way back to the present only when she talks about her daughter. "For two years now, I've had a grandson . . . He's such a joy! You should see how cute he is!"

A new controversy erupted in November of the same year when it was revealed that Roberto Del Bello, the personal secretary of the Deputy Minister of the Interior, had been convicted of membership in an armed group and served a prison sentence of four years and seven months. In December yet another scandal broke when the Minister of Social Solidarity appointed Susanna Ronconi to the National Council on Drug Addiction. Ronconi seemed to have excellent credentials in the field, on the basis of both her experience and her publications. But she had also been a member of the Red Brigades commando that in 1974 attacked an office of the Neo-Fascist Party in Padua and took the lives of two people. This time the controversy ended with her resignation. The Rome prosecutor's office also began an investigation of the minister for official misconduct: as a former terrorist, Ms.

Ronconi was prohibited from holding public office, so her appointment was illegal. She contested the judiciary's interpretation and complained that she was being "shackled to a story from thirty years ago." She added: "No one is giving any importance to what I've done since then. It's not right. It's vindictive. I do not deny my responsibility and I know that compensation for human life is not possible, but I served my sentence in full and as proof that I've changed there is the truth of the life that I've lived and the concrete commitment I've made."

On January 29, 1979, Emilio Alessandrini was killed by eight gunshots fired by two members of Prima Linea, Marco Donat Cattin and Sergio Segio, shortly after dropping off his son Marco at school. He was thirty-seven, the same age as his son is today. Marco Alessandrini is a lawyer in Pescara, his father's hometown. His father was a prosecutor who distinguished himself first for his investigations into right-wing terrorism—he uncovered the Neo-Fascists' role in the Piazza Fontana massacre and the Italian Secret Service's obstruction of the investigation into it—and then for an investigation into the left-wing terrorism of a Milan chapter of Autonomia Operaia. Marco has his father's smiling face, broad forehead, gentle manners, and passion for basketball.

Marco doesn't enjoy speaking in public, but he feels compelled to by a strong sense of duty. His speeches are remarkable for the precise and polished language he uses. "I want to help feed my country's hunger for memory." The first time he found the courage to speak out was during an interview with *Corriere della Sera*. "It's not true that time heals all wounds. My mother was thirty-four years old when they killed her husband. In a certain sense, she has never moved past that twenty-ninth of January." They had left Milan for Pescara a few days after the murder, in silence. And in silence they remained for another quarter of a century. "Today we're suffering from this rather disturbing Italian peculiarity: former terrorists elevated to the status of philosophers, writing books, granting erudite interviews. A full-fledged cultural industry has been created and we are supposed to sit back and accept it."

In the most audacious and horrifying crime of the Years of Lead, the former prime minister Aldo Moro was kidnapped by the Red Brigades on March 16, 1978, as he was being driven to Parliament. Eight weeks later, after long and fruitless negotiations, his bullet-riddled body was found in the trunk of a car in central Rome. What is often forgotten is that the gunmen also murdered five members of Moro's escort. Years later, on February 27, 2007, a TV special was broadcast titled *The Return of the Red Brigades*. In one part, the anchor, Claudio Martelli, interviewed the founder of the Red Brigades, Alberto Franceschini, at the scene of the crime on Via Fani in Rome. After decades of silence, the families of the fallen policemen wrote a letter to the columnist Corrado Augias of *La Repubblica* to describe their discomfort over that interview:

> This scene took us back thirty years, to that terrible day when our lives stopped at the same time as those of our loved ones. We were horrified to see a terrorist standing next to the plaque that commemorates the massacre. We were disgusted to hear talk of the Red Brigades at that historic place, which should be sacred to the nation and to our collective memory. Lorenzo Conti—whose father, Lando, the former mayor of Florence, was murdered by the Red Brigades in 1986—went on a hunger strike to protest the presence of former terrorists in the government. The President of the Republic, Giorgio Napolitano, implored him to suspend the strike, saying: "I want our public opinion and our politicians to remember the gravity of the terrorist attacks on democratic institutions. And I want them to remember the men who

defended these institutions with courage, making the ultimate sacrifice of their lives." Also in keeping with the head of state's remarks, we feel that it is indecent to film and present interviews of this type at commemorative sites.

In his response, Corrado Augias may have finally given the family members the understanding they were seeking.

What the letter says is perfectly true. After spending a few years in prison, terrorists implicated in the taking of human life are given back their freedom. On the release form is stamped, I believe, "time served." But the time of those whose husbands or brothers were murdered is never served, and it could never be stamped on a piece of paper. There is no getting past the disparity of treatment between those who killed and those who were killed. It goes on through the years, aggravated by the fact that the killers write memoirs, are interviewed on TV, participate in films, and occupy positions of responsibility, while no one goes to the widow of a police officer and asks her what life has been like without a husband, whether there are any children who grew up as orphans, whether the passage of time has healed the wounds, the mourning, the sorrow.

Why were they killed? Because of the dreams of a group of firebrands who were playing revolution, fooling themselves into thinking that they were the chosen ones, beautiful souls devoted to a noble utopia, without realizing that the true "children of the people," as Pasolini called them, were on the other side, the targets of their ridiculous folly.

a left-wing painter

IT TOOK A LEFT-WING PAINTER to get me to stop reading *Robinson Crusoe* twice a year. He picked it up and said, "There are lots of other books where you're not alone on a desert island after a shipwreck. They're nice. You'll like them." For security I took the novel back from him and continued to keep it next to my bed for years, but I accepted *Il giornalino di Gian Burrasca* (The Diary of Hurricane Johnny, an Italian children's classic), *Tom Sawyer* and *The Adventures of Huckleberry Finn,* and later on *David Copperfield* and the tales of an English veterinarian, James Herriot, that my grandfather gave me as a present.

At the time, I was already in elementary school, but the painter had first come into our lives while I was in kindergarten. He appeared one afternoon right before dark. We saw a man with a big headful of curls at the door and liked him instantly. We were always looking for a father figure. Nonno and our uncles did their part, but at sunset we were left alone with my mother. She would give us our baths, putting all three of us in the tub together, and we would splash around in the water. Then, when it was dark, we would be overcome by sadness. For years the night brought us nightmares and tears. The painter said his name was Tonino. Studying him carefully, I noticed that his fingers were smudged with blue tempera. After a moment of hesitation, I jumped up and put my arms around him, saying, "Tonino is mine." We sequestered him and he spent his time playing with us, wrestling and tickling us on the sofa.

He had come by to visit my mother, but she had barely enough time to give him the grilled cheese and ham sandwich that she had prepared. When he was on his way out, Luigi, who was almost three, asked him, "When are you coming back?" Caught off-guard, Tonino answered, "Tomorrow." And just like that he started coming for one hour every evening, before going off to teach illustration at the Castello Sforzesco night school. He spent all his time with us on the living room rug. Mama would look at us while leaning against the doorframe and then make him something to eat.

He entered our lives slowly, with tact and delicacy. He started to take us to Parco Sempione in the broken-down red Spider he drove and then to the planetarium and the museum of natural history. Once he showed up with a huge roll of brown packing paper and crayons, and from that moment on we spent the afternoons lying on the floor coloring.

Before long my mother's parents asked her to come by their house, alone. They needed to speak with her, and asked her to take a seat across from them at the round table in the dining room. The first to speak, with concern, was my grandmother. She asked whether it was true that a "longhair" often came to her house. My mother, embarrassed, said yes, that there was a teacher, an artist, with somewhat long curly hair, whom she spent some time with. So was it true, Nonna asked, that the painter lived in a house with many other people? "We heard about it from the children." The painter was living in a four-room apartment that he shared with a computer programmer, Baldassarre Giunta, nicknamed Sino; a cartoon artist, Antonio Dall'Osso; and a changing roster of other artists, most of them Tuscans from Lucca. For us it was a magical place, full of drawings and colors, a place where you could open the refrigerator and grab whatever you wanted, certainly less orderly than our grandparents' house. The occupants of the house—who regularly paid their rent—adopted us and even today they never miss the sad or happy moments of our lives. At weddings they always send us a shipment of Tuscan wine, and on the walls of our house there are paintings by the Tuscan painter Giuliano Natalini.

After what had happened, it's not hard to understand my grandparents' attitude. At one point they burst out, "Well, Gemma, let's call a spade a spade. He's a long-haired painter and a Communist who lives in a commune. What do you see in him? Why are you dating him?" At first my mother tried to defend him, saying that he wasn't a Communist and that there was no commune. Then she snapped and said peremptorily, "Because he loves my children and makes them laugh. I have nothing more to discuss."

My grandparents understood and made an effort to accept a person who was so unlike them. The next Sunday, they invited him to lunch. I remember a palpable tension that dissipated only thanks to the Piedmontese specialties being served, *bagna cauda* (a warm fondue-like dish of olive oil, garlic, and anchovies served with raw or cooked vegetables) and risotto, and to my mother's younger brother, Zio Attilio, who is completely bald today, but back then had a headful of curls. He broke the ice by saying something like, "They told me you were a longhair, but your hair's shorter than mine!"

Attilio was the good-luck charm of our childhood. He taught us to love bicycles and American music. He infected my brothers with his passion for motorbikes and enchanted us with his work as a fashion photographer. His studio was our refuge when we skipped school, and it was an amazing place. When you're sixteen, going from high school teachers to fashion models is a leap you don't easily forget.

The disconnect between Tonino and my grandparents was repaired so thoroughly over time that I came to see it as a model for the way Italy could be if the fences and barricades between people were to fall. They influenced each other and learned to appreciate each other, but without surrendering their guiding principles, although with the changing of the seasons they began to see eye to eye in a few areas.

We lived our lives experiencing the best of two seemingly irreconcilable worlds. We children took turns spending weekends and holidays with my grandparents, who were textile manufacturers: we went skiing in Courmayeur or hiking in Switzerland. For Easter vacation, they would take all three of us to Venice. Nonno always had a late-model Lancia. They taught us the importance of the work ethic, saving, and charity, and how to recognize a fabric blindfolded. With Mama and Tonino, who came to live with us in 1976, we traveled instead in a Fiat 127. We drove up and down Italy to discover beaches and monuments, and little by little all three of us started to breathe again, and to no longer feel threatened and lost. My brothers started to call Tonino Papà. I did not. It took me several more years, but when I did, it was because I was truly convinced that he had become our father.

Children have always been Tonino's passion. With Bruno Munari, one of Italy's greatest designers, he used to organize workshops for kids to encourage their creativity. Among his many accomplishments, he designed the peace flag—the rainbow standard that in recent years has invaded the Italian streets.

Tonino taught us how to fish, how to use a camera, how to row, to swim, to draw, to recognize the stars and the right wind for flying kites, to build sand castles, to make surfaces for playing marbles, and above all to never give up, to never take anything for granted, to fight for the things that you love.

He got up at night when we cried and invented grandiose methods for fighting our sadness. Every morning he came to wake us up with a puppet show of imaginary characters. He told little stories and made jokes. The morning became a time of the day that was not to be missed. He never tried to push Papà Gigi to the side. He sustained us during the trials and always encouraged us to keep his memory alive.

In December 1982, in a small church that overlooks the Gulf of Tigullio in Liguria, my mother and Tonino were married, and two years later our fourth brother, Uber, was born. With his arrival, our story turned another page: in the city records and on the mailbox there were now three last names, sometimes making it very difficult to explain things. It wasn't always easy, especially for Uber, whose life was weighed down by a heavy and never-ending story. He was little, still in nursery school, when one night before going to bed he said, "Mama, I don't know what to do. I love my brothers and I'm sad that their father is dead, but if it hadn't happened I wouldn't have been born." During his first year of high school, one of his teachers organized an assembly about Adriano Sofri, who had been convicted of instigating my father's murder, but had gone through multiple trials with varying outcomes. The only speaker invited was Guido Viale, the former leader of Lotta Continua. My brother asked why the opposite side wasn't represented, and he was told, "Why, do you want those poor guys to go to jail?" He came home and asked for everything to be explained to him, to be given all the details of the story. Uber wanted to take the floor at the assembly, so that at least one voice would remember Luigi Calabresi, even if Uber wasn't his son. We thanked him, then my mother asked him to stay home that day, so that he would miss the assembly. We never felt that he was different from us. Now we were four and our stories blended into one.

And so Sunday after Sunday, year after year, we learned all the ordinary things that should belong to a shared heritage: that there were two Italys, each with its relative merits, and with good people on both sides. We learned that people from the right, the left, and the center could join together in laughter, affection, good conversation, debate, discomfort, and sadness. I quickly realized that our family was a little different, in a good way that defied stereotypes. For example, when my mother and I went to an art opening at a "leftist" gallery, we might be greeted by a brief chill in the air. We never worried because after a while the climate would change. Other people would start to see us as individuals rather than symbols, regard us with compassion, and maybe even start to question some of their own assumptions.

I've always compared what happened to a shipwreck. Suddenly you lose everything; you find yourself tossing about in dark and deep water. Sometimes the disaster could have been predicted because of an approaching storm, but there are also sudden leaks in the boat, icebergs, killer whales. While the shipwreck that befell my father should have been foretold—a glance at the papers from those years tells you everything—some dramas are still unexpected and unpredictable.

The most telling aspect of this image is the aftermath: you can be adrift for years or for your entire life. You can end up on a desert island and choose to remain there. Many victims of terrorism talk about their experience lucidly, saying that they could never again turn the page of the calendar, that their pain and anger has chained them to that moment. It's hard to break away from it of your own will. Some people choose an island that allows them to survive. Many run as far away as they can get.

We have to thank my mother for having had the courage to allow Tonino to help her, and fate, for bringing us into a large extended family. My mother is the fourth of seven children. Her sisters and brothers never let us down. We called one set the "Carlos," a name that identified eight people: my oldest uncle, Carlo; his wife, Carla; and six children. In their midst you were diluted, you became part of something bigger, and differences were erased. The only problem is that they are all blue-eyed blonds or redheads. We were like dark spots: you could pick us out immediately. Then there were our African cousins, born at the source of the Blue Nile, as they used to say, the children of two courageous doctors, Gigi and Mirella, who helped to found a hospital in Gulu, in northern Uganda. They captivated us with stories that lasted for hours, about playing games in the savannah, about zebras and giraffes.

It's exhausting to be rescued from the waves. The difficulties cannot always be avoided, diluted, transformed, or ignored. When the problem was too great and the decision delicate we all sat together around the kitchen table. It's where we made our most important decisions. It's where we gathered even after we children had grown up and left home. It's where a few years ago, attached to a poster of a Picasso exhibit, Tonino left a poem for us to find, explaining something that had never been said.

Father
one day
after the other,
for love
elected,
not for bread.

Loved
right away,
mysteriously
mine.

we shall love again

IN THE AFTERMATH OF SEPTEMBER 11, 2001, the *New York Times* began to publish short biographies of the people who had died in the Twin Towers. They were written with passion and filled with life and color. I was amazed to read in one of the first to appear the story of a stockbroker who had only recently achieved his crowning dream of buying a Porsche. Because of his cigar habit, however, it had immediately become filled with smoke and ash. I wondered what type of tribute this was supposed to be and whether it was appropriate to remember the victim of a terrorist attack in this way. I tried to imagine a more traditional obituary, containing expressions such as "wonderful father," "loved by all," "model employee," "citizen above reproach." What if such expressions were repeated hundreds of times, until all 2,603 of the victims had been remembered? No one would have read them. No one would have clipped them from the newspaper. No one would have conserved the memories. But I can still remember the story of a woman whose office was on one of the top floors and who was happy because she could see her son's school from up there. For it is the little things—full and realistic recollections—that keep memory alive, not rhetoric.

One way of preserving difficult memories is to hold long and boring ceremonies with bureaucratic rituals that go on for hours and a litany of ornate words of appreciation and a plethora of descriptions such as "barbarously struck down in the prime of his youth by the ignominious hand of an assassin." Such ceremonies are supposed to keep memory alive, but they are all wrong, especially for an audience of schoolchildren. They shouldn't have to drown in names and quotations that are a mystery to them, and they are easily bored if they don't understand what a speaker is talking about. Parents and teachers sometimes argue in response, "But young people have the duty to know . . . They should remember." So tell them something that's worth the trouble of remembering.

When I go to these encounters, I talk about my father as a normal man, not as a hero or a Martian. I talk about his weaknesses and eccentricities. After all, these "heroes" were ordinary people, defined by their limitless passion for the things they do. They are people you could identify with, who loved their work and did it wholeheartedly. Like Emilio Alessandrini, who was killed for the "crime" of making the Milan prosecutor's office more efficient. Or Luigi Marangoni, who wanted his hospital to be run properly, and couldn't bear for blood banks to be damaged or for orderlies in the morgue to cut deals with undertakers.

On January 29, 2005, twenty-six years after Alessandrini's death, I was at the high school in Pescara where he had studied. His son Marco and I each spoke about our parents. He captivated the children when he told them about the last Christmas before the murder. He wanted them to understand the void that violence leaves in the everyday life of a family. "We had just returned home after visiting various relatives, but I absolutely had to see the cartoon *Goldrake* on a color TV. So my father put his coat back on and we went back to my maternal grandparents so that I could. He let me get my way every time. There was a great sense of complicity between us. They say it's not good for your father to be your friend, but this is exactly why I loved him and why I'm so sorry to have lost him."

One month earlier I had paid a visit to the high school where my father had studied, San Leone Magno of Rome, which had decided to dedicate a plaque to him on a wall of the courtyard. I went with his older sister, my aunt Wanda. Speeches were given by the deputy police chief, the prefect, who had known my father well, and the school principal, who depicted him as a model student. "You could already tell back then that he would be a hero." My aunt whispered in my ear, "You wouldn't believe how much trouble he got into! He even flunked his senior year and had to finish high school somewhere else." At the end they asked me if there was anything that I wished to say to the students. From their faces, I could see that all those stories from the 1970s didn't mean a thing to them, so I changed the tone. "Let's be honest. He wasn't exactly a model student. As a matter of fact he was a catastrophe! He even flunked." The students started to pay more attention and to look at me in amazement. So I said what was in my heart. "The people that they introduce to you as heroes were ordinary people, but with a great love for democracy and the Republic. They did their work with passion." I didn't have the courage to add that he hadn't graduated from their school. I could already see the pained look on the face of the principal, who probably wasn't aware of the fact, so I thanked them and directed everyone to the buffet.

Every now and then there are unexpected moments of pure magic. On May 23, 2003, the eleventh anniversary of the assassination of Giovanni Falcone, Italy's most famous anti-Mafia judge, about a hundred wives, children, and mothers of hero-victims of our history came from every part of Italy to Mestre, on the outskirts of Venice. They came without fanfare, learning of the event by word of mouth. They came to remember, to try to give life to a shared memory that included the victims of Mafia violence, terrorism, and massacres. They were joined by students from the Venetian high schools. A joint effort by the national policemen's union and a small volunteer association, this initiative became an unprecedented ritual for the sharing of these experiences. The audience gathered in the theater that day listened to the families' testimony in hushed silence.

Giuseppe Esposito was five years old in 1978 when the Red Brigades of Genoa killed his father, Antonio, on the municipal bus that was taking him to the Nervi police station. His son describes him affectionately but in an understated way, describing how he got to know his father through newspaper clippings and family friends. "He was a meticulous and thorough investigator, more Carthusian monk than policeman chasing bandits." But he didn't stop at personal memories. He also mentioned that the National Association of Partisans had decided to add Esposito's name to the list of those who had died for freedom.

Not far away, three women were listening to him, filled with emotion, thinking of their own sons or husbands. They had arrived together on the train from Rome. Maria Bitti, the widow of Marshal Mariano Romiti, shook her head. Her husband had been killed by the Red Brigades, while he was waiting for the bus in a working-class suburb on the day of their fourth son's fifteenth birthday. Next to her was Eugenia Vergani, who had lost her son in a Red Brigade kidnapping on St. Valentine's Day in 1987. The third woman was the widow of Domenico Ricci, the driver of Aldo Moro, who was killed during the kidnapping on Via Fani. They had the painful and depressing job of sifting through their memories, and they took the floor to explain their feelings to the young people gathered for the occasion. They talked about days spent searching through family albums for a photograph that would pierce the numbness that had engulfed them. They asked the audience to understand, and they showed how their sorrow is renewed every time they talk about it: each of them wept with anger and disbelief, saying they could find no peace, in part because the list of victims continues to grow.

Manlio Milani summarized the overarching theme of the event. "Through this assembly, by keeping these memories alive, we can recall the people who were lost and the reasons for their disappearance." On May 27, 1974, he and his wife, Livia, were at dinner in Brescia at the home of Clementina Calzari and Alberto Trebeschi. The next day, a bomb exploded during an anti-Fascist protest in the center of the city, at the Piazza della Loggia, taking the lives of eight people, including Alberto, Clementina, and Livia. "All three of them were teachers. They helped to found the school of CGIL, one of Italy's three largest trade unions. For twenty years, we were always together. They died together, struck by the bomb. I am the only one who survived, together with Giorgio, the son of Clem and Alberto, who was one and a half years old at the time and the projection of our hopes." His words are filled with regret for a lost world that was denied a future. "Alberto and I were members of the Italian Communist Party. We were active in a cultural circle that included a cinema section. On September 11, 1973, the day that Salvador Allende, the president of Chile, was murdered during a military coup d'état, we were at the Pesaro Film Festival. There were some Latin American directors—a really beautiful group of people—and we lived the Chilean tragedy with them. The four of us were politically active, fighting for good schools for the children of factory workers, but we also had dinner parties and went on vacations together." Milani is the head of the Association of the Families of the Fallen and he directs the House of Memory in Brescia, a well-run center that organizes lecture series for schools, most recently on the rhetoric of the 1970s. He inherited the burden of testifying, a duty he never shirks. "I still get together with Giorgio. Today he is a big, good-looking, intelligent boy. He was raised by Alberto's twin brother. Every time I see him I tell him, 'I'm getting old, but I'm still here. When you're ready we can talk about it.' But he can't, and every time I ask he shakes his head no."

What we need in Italy is a place like the memorial in Washington, D.C., dedicated to the 58,260 victims of the Vietnam War. It's made of black marble. The visitors' faces are mirrored in the engraved names, which can be touched, caressed with the fingers, transferred onto a sheet of paper by rubbing a pencil on top. It's a place of collective memory. It would be nice if there were something of this kind in Italy to remember the victims of left- and right-wing terrorism.

Attempts at a monument have been made at a couple of places in Rome. The Casa del Jazz is an estate confiscated from the cashier of the Magliana Gang, an organized crime syndicate based in Rome that was particularly active in the 1970s. The villa has an amazing building and two acres of parks with Mediterranean pines, in the middle of which is a large stela with the names of 683 innocent victims of the Mafia from 1893 to the present. On Sunday mornings, concert evenings, or moonlit nights, it is always filled with people who have stopped by to read, to chat, to comment. At the Leadership Academy in the Flaminio neighborhood, there is a memorial to policemen who have fallen in the line of duty. All the names are there, engraved on illuminated plates. Unfortunately, it's a place that's difficult to reach.

After years of talk, it might finally become a reality: a "Day of Memory" dedicated to the victims of terrorism and massacres. A bill has been presented to the Chamber of Deputies according to which, on the Day of Memory, municipalities can host cere-monies, events, meetings, and moments of silence in public and at the schools to build a shared memory. The suggested date for the commemoration is May 9, the anniversary of the murder of Aldo Moro. An alternative date is March 16, when Moro was kidnapped and five members of his police escort were massa-cred on Via Fani. The Association of Victims of Massacres sug-gested December 12, the date of Piazza Fontana—the event, they emphasize, that triggered everything else—to give the com-memoration the proper chronological framework.

When I think of Aldo Moro, I think of his heartbreaking let-ters from prison, of his gentleness and sensitivity toward his family. In his final letter to his wife, he wrote,

My dear Noretta,

I fear that my possibilities are running out and, unless there is a miracle, that I am near the point at which I shall con-clude this human experience . . . how I want to hold you close and express to you all the sweetness I feel, mixed though it is with bitterness, for having had the gift of a life with you, so rich with love and deep understanding . . . Be well and try to be as tranquil as you can. We shall see each other again. We shall meet again. We shall love again.

lost opportunities

THE PIAZZA FONTANA MASSACRE took place forty years ago, making it closer chronologically to the rise of Nazism than to the fall of Saddam Hussein. The time has come to consign it to history, together with the period of bloodshed that was ushered in on that afternoon. The time has come to speak of those years more calmly, to understand what happened and why. But too many truths are missing, too many crimes unaccounted for, too many victims still awaiting justice. Every time that Italy seeks closure to this painful era, there is a public outcry driven by reasons of convenience and self-interest.

Today people are still asking the whereabouts of the perpetrators of massacres that took the lives of 150 people, as well as questioning the complicit silence in which the history of red terrorism remains enshrouded.

Difficult though it may seem, I think we can and must turn the page, but let us not forget that each page has two sides: we cannot read only the side dedicated to terrorists and their strategies: we must also and above all read the other side, about the victims.

Can someone like Manlio Milani agree to turn the page? A survivor of the Piazza della Loggia massacre in Brescia, he is still wondering why the woman he loved was murdered, and who was responsible for it. What about the people who are still awaiting compensatory damages from the state? Who are awaiting payment for treatment to take care of injuries they've suffered for decades? Who feel that the truth—about who is responsible, who colluded—is still being hidden from them? Who see the murderers of their father, brother, son, wife, or husband giving speeches at universities, on television, at conferences? How can we expect clear-headed judgment from those who feel forgotten, brushed aside, defeated? How can you ask them for the courage of clemency?

We must begin with the victims: their memories and their need for truth. Their demands for justice, assistance, help, and sensitivity should finally be fulfilled. By the government, politicians, and even the television stations, newspapers, and civil society. It would be to everyone's benefit to have a country that is able to turn the page with serenity.

President Napolitano understands this. He feels the need. His predecessor, Carlo Azeglio Ciampi, worked to unify the collective memory of Italians, to rebuild a concept of *patria* as a home where everyone can find a place. Napolitano has used this idea as his starting point, but he seems to feel a special urgency to heal the wounds. Despite a political class that is always looking for wedge issues, polemics, and divisiveness, he advances full speed ahead, forcing others to follow him.

In his year-end message in Rome, he spoke of respect for the memory of the victims. He did the same in Milan and in Bologna, where he remembered Marco Biagi, and as the professor's family noted favorably, the climate in the city changed. Then he chose to write to *La Repubblica* after its publication of a letter from the family members of the men in Aldo Moro's escort, to emphasize that he fully agreed with their words: "The legitimate reinsertion into society of perpetrators of terrorist acts who have made their reckoning with justice should be the occasion for an explicit recognition of the unjustifiable criminal nature of the terrorist attack on the state and on its representatives and servants, and should be accompanied by public behavior inspired by the greatest discretion and propriety."

Today very few terrorists are left in prison. Most have been released. Think of the biggest crimes and then do a roll call. There is a widespread sense that the terrorists were the beneficiaries of a certain leniency and were released without making a deep and lasting contribution to the truth. Instead, the state should agree to commute a terrorist's sentence only in exchange for a complete confession and an admission of guilt.

We should take the high road and leave the polemics behind. Instead, tired rituals are repeated. If a memorial tablet is placed for Calabresi, then demands come for a school to be named after Pinelli. If at the offices of the provincial government a hall is dedicated to Marco Biagi, then the reply comes that it should be associated with Massimo D'Antona, and that both names have to be present, in a tit-for-tat approach to commemoration that ultimately creates the false illusion that Biagi and D'Antona belonged to two different sides, thereby renewing divisions, preconceptions, and venom.

The state fell prey to these same sterile polemics when—to avoid losing a civil suit for its failure to grant Biagi an escort—it made an out-of-court settlement to award compensatory damages to the widow and children. The amount it agreed to pay was much higher than required by the law on the victims of terrorism. Here the state paid for its shortcomings, which ultimately cost the life of a professor, and through the settlement it took responsibility for the needs of the victims' families.

To repress rather than to remember is a lost opportunity in a country that is short of role models.

Victims' rights cannot be a private matter between the state and individual citizens. Italy needs a widespread sensitivity, a collective feeling. It is still a struggle here to utter an unambiguous condemnation of political violence. The terrorists have not been repudiated as the murderers they were. All too often, they have been described as underdogs, people who waged a battle of ideas that they were unable to win. Investigations into the latest followers of the Red Brigades in 2007 showed one thing clearly: that the younger generation is still responsive to the message of the terrorists.

The media bears a special responsibility for this state of affairs. The newspapers and television networks show too little scruple in training the spotlight on former terrorists, in giving them a stage in even the most inadvisable or inappropriate circumstances. Most disturbing and dangerous are the standard interviews: the terrorists are almost never reminded of their crimes and responsibilities. This is unacceptable, especially if they have been invited for the purpose of discussing the Years of Lead. The press usually introduces Sergio Segio, for example, as a representative of the Gruppo Abele, a social services outreach center, and almost never as a founder of the terrorist organization Prima Linea and the convicted killer of two judges, Guido Galli and Emilio Alessandrini. More often than not, Anna Laura Braghetti, the terrorist who killed Vittorio Bachelet at the University of Rome with seven bullets and participated in the kidnapping of Aldo Moro, is described as a "coordinator of social services for detainees."

A romantic idea of terrorism is being broadcast. This is especially true when reporters cover some of the more recent outbreaks of Red Brigade violence. The media compares these episodes unfavorably to the "armed struggle" of the 1970s, which they claim was sustained by ideas and a revolutionary project.

One woman has reflected more deeply and articulately than anyone else on Italy's inability to engage in public grieving. Carole Beebe, an American, met Ezio Tarantelli in Boston, at the student center of the Massachusetts Institute of Technology. He was a student of the prominent economist Franco Modigliani, while she was a Ph.D. candidate in English literature at Brandeis. They used to go out dancing together. They were married in 1970 and she later followed him to Italy, where they had one son, Luca. Tarantelli was murdered in Rome at the university where he taught economics on March 27, 1985. There were two gunmen, but only one was identified and convicted. "The other could even be sitting right next to me at a movie theater one night."

A therapist and a teacher of English literature and psychoanalysis at the University of Rome, Carole Tarantelli was also a left-wing member of Parliament for three sessions. "Italy has been unable to articulate not only grief, but even a single thought about terrorism. It is neither willing nor capable of really thinking about it. Italy has never engaged in a complete reckoning." On the possibility of the nation moving on without owning up to responsibilities toward the victims, she is absolute. "In Italy an illusion has been making headway that is equivalent to the terrorists' fantasy that what they did can be overcome as if nothing happened. This is not a question of good or bad will. It's a simple question of reality, because the effects of their acts can still be felt. They can be felt in the people who survived, and they can be felt every day in the absence of the people that they killed. Terrorism will not be over as long as my son Luca—who carries the marks of it—is alive. Its negative effects continue in our life every day; we cannot forget about it."

I think of the life of Ezio Tarantelli and of what was robbed from us, of everything that he had to offer. Of the opportunities that terrorism took away from our country.

the rules of the kitchen

FOR YEARS I filed away newspaper clippings, wire dispatches, documents, and notes, accumulating tons of words, controversies, and rage. I kept this strange archive in boxes, colored backpacks, and an old blue Samsonite suitcase from the 1970s. On different occasions last year, I opened them all up. The dust burned my eyes while I struggled to find a thread that would connect the thousand of articles and columns on the trials, appeals, ad hoc laws, petitions, proclamations, controversies over pardons, hunger and water strikes, and infighting among exterrorists. I read and reread the statements by two former members of Lotta Continua, the journalist Giampiero Mughini and the writer Erri De Luca, when they finally came clean about what happened to my father. Mughini went so far as to admit, "I think that a Lotta Continua commando killed Calabresi." For his part, De Luca asserted, "Any of us could have killed Calabresi." Their admissions provoked a furious backlash from their former comrades, who immediately denied their claims.

The day came when I didn't know what to do with all these yellowing files anymore. Whenever I opened them up, hours would go by as I searched for their underlying meaning. I wanted to think that they would help me write a book that finally explained exactly what had happened. Then I realized that it was a hopeless endeavor, and that I, too, would continue to be a prisoner of these petty, squalid polemics. Unless I took a major step. So I got up my courage, took a deep breath, and in an almost unconscious leap, like jumping off a cliff, I threw everything away. Years of nocturnal labors ended up in the trash. The only thing I kept was a blue file with the things that seemed most shocking. After a moment of panic, I felt lighter. Today I use the same blue suitcase to hold trays of slides from family vacations.

There are also slides from the summer in Liguria in 1988 when an evening news station informed us that sixteen years after the murder of my father, a series of arrests had been made. I had just turned eighteen. Until that moment, the biggest topic in the month of July had been over what time I had to be home at night: I argued that my curfew days were well over, but somehow I couldn't prevail. And then all of a sudden the whole family was catapulted into a story we thought had been relegated to the past and become almost a private matter.

On July 20, Leonardo Marino, a former Lotta Continua militant, after having turned himself in voluntarily to the police, confessed to taking part in the assassination of my father. He claimed that he had been the driver, and he named three other Lotta Continua members as his accomplices: Ovidio Bompressi, Giorgio Pietrostefani, and Adriano Sofri. This set in motion a series of trials, appeals, Supreme Court decisions, and requests for clemency that would last well over a decade.

The immediate result was a media frenzy and a complete disruption of my family's life. My mother was called by the magistrates in Milan for questioning. Threatening phone calls started to come in at night. Journalists waited outside our door, and a group of policemen from the antiterrorism squad stood around in the yard.

We had no preconceived ideas about the men who had been arrested, despite all the news coming out in the papers about them. For hours we sat around the kitchen table discussing what we should do. No one felt like cooking, so we survived on focaccia with cheese from the bakery. In the end, we decided to apply to join the proceedings as a civil party.

Little did we know how many long, mortifying years we would end up spending in the courtroom. Today my mother always says that when the final bill on her life is drawn up, these years should be deducted. But they were also educational. For one thing, they convinced me to abandon law school. Every day, as I was descending the immense staircase of the Palazzo di Giustizia, the huge Fascist-style courthouse of Milan, to Corso di Porta Vittoria, I used to ask myself, What am I doing? Am I studying so I can come back inside here every morning? And then would I ever find the necessary peace of mind to be a judge? I made the happy decision to transfer to the history department.

The trials forced me to pay closer attention to the newspapers. Although I found the news biased, I did become good friends with some of the journalists, and we used to talk for hours outside the courtroom. The profession itself intrigued me more and more. My classmates and I also developed a passion for politics. Every Monday evening, we would go to the town hall to observe the council's proceedings. Major changes were about to take place that would eventually shake up the entire postwar political order in Italy. In the city, a web of corruption was uncovered that could be traced to the highest levels of government. The ensuing scandal, which became known as Tangentopoli, or Kickback City, brought down one of the most powerful men in

Italy, Benito Craxi, and with him the Socialist Party that had long ruled the city and the country. In its wake, a new political force sprung up, the separatist Northern League, which wanted to wrest power away from Rome and create stronger regional government.

I became involved in grass-roots movements and worked on the 1993 mayoral campaign of Nando Dalla Chiesa, the son of General Carlo Alberto Dalla Chiesa, the hero who had helped defeat the Red Brigades in the late 1970s and was ignominiously assassinated when he tried to apply the same techniques to halting the Sicilian Mafia. One day at a covered market we ran into a representative of the Northern League who later became speaker of the Milan city council. She saw us enter and shouted into the megaphone, "Here are the friends of the terrorists. The terrorists will not rule Milan."

In the end, the Northern League's candidate, Marco Formentini, won the mayoral election and the Socialists were driven from power. All around us, the city and the political climate were changing, but the trials continued unabated. The hero of the kickback scandal, Judge Antonio Di Pietro, railed against political corruption. In the courthouse corridors, we saw his rise and fall. Still the trials went on. In Rome Silvio Berlusconi, the leader of a new party, Forza Italia, became the prime minister, and still we were at the courthouse.

At the Palazzo di Giustizia, my schoolmates never failed me. They took turns keeping the family company and listening and debating: Andrea, Marcello, Bea, Enzo, Saida, Larry, and Silvia. For years I've remembered their generosity, their physical presence, and their sharing of the difficult moments. It still continues today, and it is something for which I am grateful.

Two people whose lives were linked by the same tragedy, the murder of General Dalla Chiesa by the Mafia, telephone us every year on May 17, the anniversary of my father's death, and after every verdict from the many trials of my father's killers. They are his son, Nando, and Gianmaria Setti Carraro, the brother of Manuela, the general's young wife, who was killed with him. There is no one else like them. We used to tell a family joke, saying that they were substitutes for the government, which was nowhere to be found.

My mother developed her own clear-cut rules on how we should deal with all the media attention: never polemicize, never speak too much, show respect and kindness to everyone, and above all, trust in the judiciary. "We are not seeking revenge. We are seeking justice, and we will respect the verdicts that come," she told us clearly at dawn on the day of the first hearing, while we were sitting in the kitchen. "I did everything possible for you to grow up without grudges or hatred. The last thing I want is to ruin that now." She spent many nights sitting at Luigi's bedside to comfort him. After a detailed account of the morning of the homicide was given in court, we heard her speaking to him that night in a soft voice for hours. He was looking for a thread to tie him to the present, to an idea of the future. He didn't want to lose himself, to start wallowing in sorrow over the fact that he'd never known his father, that he was born too late. They talked and talked, helping him get a grip on his anger, transforming his suffering into something more manageable.

Luigi's feelings are sharper, more raw. He has always been very direct in telling Paolo and me, "The difference between us is that he never held me in his arms." Mama remembers the leap she felt in her belly when she received the news of the murder and she understands him. "When I see his anger, I feel exactly what I felt that day." Every now and then he hurtles into my mother's home in a fury. Like the time he learned that Adriano Sofri was at the Palio of Siena, a traditional horse race in medieval costume, at the window where the government officials were seated, being welcomed and introduced as a celebrity by the mayor. Or the time he was holding a page torn out of a magazine with a picture of Sofri in a boat on the pond in Rome's Villa Borghese gardens, with his son and granddaughter. "Here's the difference, don't forget it: our father didn't get this chance to become a grandfather." At that point, my mother took him aside and tried to console him.

On April 27, 1990, the Third Court of Assizes of Milan, presided over by Manlio Minale, entered into chambers. Five days later, on May 2, the sentence was read. I remember the paralyzing wait. We couldn't help it. The energy needed to keep up any pretense of normality was gone, and we spent the last two days alternating between the sofa and the bed. I was sleeping in the same bedroom as Paolo and I remember that afternoon, prostrate, immobile, as if we were undone by the summer heat. Later that afternoon, someone attempted a joke, but in the end it was impossible to break the tension. We were all waiting for the telephone to ring, and we all raced to it every time it did. Finally our lawyers notified us that the sentence was about to be read, so we rushed to the courthouse. When we realized that the defendants had been convicted, my mother started to cry. I asked her why. I thought it must have been the memories. She caught me completely off-guard. "For Bompressi's daughter. Today she has lost her father."

The time arrived for the Court of Cassation to confirm the verdict. Mama was inflexible with the lawyers. "We are not coming to Rome. It's the court of final appeal and it's better for a widow and orphans to be outside the hall, to avoid putting any emotional pressure on the judges."

After the many trials were over, the time began for the long and heated debates over whether to grant clemency. My family's position has always been the same, and we have repeated it to every President of the Republic: we will accept any decision taken in the general interest, but we ask that the sentences themselves be respected. It would be unacceptable to grant a pardon that resembled a new instance of justice, that could be interpreted or presented as a reparation or acquittal.

We take no pleasure in the incarceration of the convicts: it never gave us back anything, nor has it ever been a source of consolation for us. What matters are the sentences, the state's commitment to seek the truth, to do justice. At home we have always been irritated when someone has asked us to approve or deny parole or a pardon. We reject the medieval notion that the victim's relatives should decide the fate of the convict. The responsibility for the decision lies not with the family but with the courts and Parliament, on the basis of the legal code. These are not private matters. Justice is the duty of the state. Despite my family's position of absolute neutrality, we are often cited as if we were in favor of clemency by representatives of every part of the political spectrum fighting for the release of convicts. From the right, I remember getting a telephone call from a group of Forza Italia members of Parliament. They had been asked to sign a document that was supposed to end the wrangling between the Ministry of Justice and the president's office over whether to grant clemency to Bompressi. They wanted to know whether it was true, as they had heard from their coordinator, that my family had approved the text. I said that it was not, adding that it was not right to lay at our door the responsibility for decisions that would be unpopular with the electorate.

From the left, I remember being invited to the headquarters of the Democratic Party of the Left. The justice adviser very politely proposed to me a type of exchange. He said that the time had come to allow the clemency to go forward, just as the time has come to rehabilitate the figure of my father. Each of us could do his part. We left each other respectfully, but I told him that I didn't see a moral equivalency between the two, and above all that granting clemency was not our responsibility.

One evening, shortly before writing a letter to the newspaper *Il Foglio*, explaining that the time was ripe for granting a pardon to Sofri, Silvio Berlusconi invited me to dinner at his home on Via del Plebiscito in Rome. His political adviser Gianni Letta was also at the table. The prime minister had just arrived from Brussels and he had a stomachache. The only thing he ate was yogurt. He took two tablespoons of an antacid and explained to me what he had in mind. He spoke to me about the importance of symbolic gestures, about the need to detoxify the climate around the judicial system, and he asked me whether my family and I were open to agreeing on a gesture of clemency. He mentioned that he had met my father and he spoke of him with great respect and esteem. But I told him that this was not feasible, that you couldn't ask it of my mother, that if he thought it was right to take a step in this direction then we would respect his decision, but that we did not want to be involved. I remember that he took it badly, tapping his fingers on the table and rubbing his jaw. Then his chef Michele's gelato arrived and he forgot all about the acidity in his stomach. I said good-bye to him and took the stairs. Letta accompanied me to the courtyard and said, "You've done the right thing. This time I do not agree with him, and he knows it."

Then came the medal, and more important, the words of President Ciampi: "We have rediscovered memory." "Better late than never" is what we said in my family, and we truly meant it. It might be commonplace, but it fits the occasion. I can't bear the malcontents, the conspiracy theorists, the people who say, "After all this time . . ." My reply is that we should accept it for what it is, in its most obvious aspect. The medal, like the commemorative stamp, was an important recognition. And the plaques on Via Cherubini and at the offices of the province of Milan will be, when they are finally in place. All our lives we thought it was unjust not to remember him at the place where he was killed, and not to recognize his sacrifice with a medal. Now there is one. Mama held it in her hand. The president pinned it on her jacket. This is what matters. Not being able to appreciate this would be a terrible loss. You have to try not to remain stuck, mummified, repeating the liturgy of mourning ad infinitum. That is not how you commemorate the deceased. We wanted to keep Luigi Calabresi alive, redeem his memory, clear him of the mud, and give him justice. So to see his smiling face on the stamps, on the envelopes, at the tobacconist, at the post office, on police calendars—I even found his face at a Chinese restaurant in Milan!—is a victory. And we are not interested in— and are indeed irritated by—arguments such as "They only did it in order to . . ." "In order to what?" "It's a maneuver to keep you quiet, to sugarcoat the pill, to then grant a pardon to Sofri and company." That's certainly possible, but we cannot pretend not to see that, even if this is the case, the government's first thought was for us, the rehabilitation of his memory. And are these things not real, visible, concrete? So we accept them rather than ruin everything with conspiracy theories. Mama's smile on the morning of the medal was real. The peace of mind it gave her compensated for many bitter moments. To ruin everything, to poison these gestures, would have been stupid, unproductive, and above all ungenerous.

After the trials, I never saw Sofri, Bompressi, or Pietrostefani again.

It's the summer of 2002 and I am visiting Paris as a correspondent for *La Stampa*. The French elections are taking place, and will be won by President Jacques Chirac's Union for a Popular

Movement. The soccer World Cup is being played in Japan and Korea. One afternoon I have a coffee on the terrace of the *Le Monde* building with the French correspondent for my paper, Cesare Martinetti, and a reporter who writes for *Il Giornale* of Milan. The latter invites us to watch the match on television at his house that night. I accept immediately and thank him. I have no desire to stay at the hotel by myself. Cesare jumps up. "Unfortunately, we can't. We have a previous engagement." Somewhat naively, I insist that he's wrong, that we have nothing scheduled for that night, and that I would be very happy to go. Cesare adopts a stern tone that I have never heard him use. "I'm afraid we cannot, I assure you." I take it badly. We go down to the street and for a while neither of us speaks. Then he explains. "In that house, on the armchair in front of the TV set, you would have found Pietrostefani, the man convicted of organizing your father's murder. He plops himself down and doesn't move. I didn't want you to have to go through that." He's right. That evening we don't watch the match. We stroll along the Seine deep into the night, conversing about the trials and about my father.

14.

apologies

BENEATH THE PORTICOES of Via Valdonica, in the center of Bologna, the pedestrians lower their voices. Instinct tells me to hold my breath. The air is thick, almost motionless. The street is narrow, as if the overwhelming sadness and the senseless act that provoked it were still there, trapped between the narrow walls, beneath the vault, unable to blend with the sky. You cannot help but look around in search of the bicycle of the professor, of Marco Biagi, who was gunned down on March 19, 2002. Walking on these stones seems to be almost sacrilegious, but every day his wife and children, who still live here, do just that, courageously. They did not run away. Despite the polemics, the insults, the lack of understanding.

The story of Marco Biagi's murder is a story of madness. But it is also a cautionary tale about the power of language. About the lighthearted, then careless, and finally irresponsible use of words. About the web that can be woven from insinuations, remarks, writings, graffiti, leaflets, malicious sentences, and stubborn silences, a web that is strong enough to trap a person's life.

It does not take a mastermind to do this. All it takes is the collusion of petty, apparently guiltless behavior by the many. It is through just such complicity that the identity of a center-left professor was distorted so badly that he came to be seen as a negative symbol of the center-right government.

Marco's wife, Marina Orlandi, understood exactly what was happening, as did he. Together they looked for a way to break out of this web and end this complicity. They wept over the attacks on his reputation and the death threats. They appealed for and even demanded protection. The government responded by ignoring the request, closing the door in his face, and treating him with frosty toleration. The conclusion was preordained. Marco Biagi, an adviser to the Ministry of Labor, was condemned to death by the terrorists, for the crime of trying to reform the Italian labor laws. The same destiny had befallen his predecessor, Massimo D'Antona, who was shot to death in Rome three years earlier, on May 20, 1999.

I knew about D'Antona from an insider, the Minister of Labor's spokesperson, Caterina, who later became my wife. In the evening, she would talk to me about this Massimo D'Antona, who was writing the Labor Reform Act, about the file folders he would bring with him from his house on Via Salaria, about the last time she had seen him at the ministry. Then I remember the morning of May 20, the immediate sense that the demons had returned to strike at the center of Rome. Not far away from Via Salaria, on Via Po, is the head office of the magazine *L'espresso*. I called there immediately and blurted out to the editor in chief, Giampaolo Pansa, "It's happening again. They're back. We've seen this all before." His answer was succinct. "I have the same sensation."

Rainfall at the commemoration. Feelings that I know all too well. Uniformed men every morning and every night waiting for Caterina to kick-start her moped or park it downstairs. It was in this period that she spoke to me about Marco Biagi, who was completing D'Antona's work in the days after the murder, to bring it to the Council of the European Union in Brussels. According to schedule. A posthumous homage to D'Antona and his life's work.

Marina Orlandi remembers every moment. "On the day that D'Antona was killed, Marco was in Rome. He, too, was working for the Minister of Labor, Antonio Bassolino, in the Massimo D'Alema government. My husband phoned and told me, 'I won't be coming back to Bologna today. I'll see you on Friday.' It was Wednesday. I begged him to come home immediately. I cried and shouted. He told me no, that he had to finish preparing the document, that they wanted it ready for the press conference. I couldn't talk him out of it. So I asked him at least not to participate in the press conference. I didn't want them to see him. He respected my wish; at least he agreed to that. I remember the anguish that began then. At night I would get up and look out the windows. For a few days, I saw a white minivan parked downstairs in the small square. It became the symbol of my fear, of our fragility."

But the precautions were useless, well outmaneuvered by an ideological hatred that even today contaminates any attempt to revise Italian labor law.

"My husband was not right-wing. He was a Socialist, but he chose to continue working at the ministry when the government changed and Roberto Maroni of the Northern League became his new boss. From that moment on, his life became harder and harder, and he was slowly but surely isolated: he was working for the enemy. Life in Bologna became difficult for us. Marco's atrocious suffering in the last months of his life stemmed from the depiction of him as a person other than who he really was. He would say, 'They've cordoned me off from polite society.'"

Marina Orlandi lives in a house filled with plants, memories, and Chinese stamps. She has no wish to name names or draw up lists of the good and the bad. She prefers to look to the future, and hopes that the Marco Biagi Foundation can be a place "where pride of place is given to dialogue and constructive criticism, indepth and unbiased study." The same way that she had envisioned it, together with her husband, the evening before they killed him. "We spoke for a long time about what he was doing to safeguard as much as possible young people, women, the least protected strata of the workforce who already had it tough, and who were very likely to have an even harder go of it. He wanted to keep going, with boyish enthusiasm, despite the fact that he felt isolated and in danger. Twenty-four hours later, he was killed. That night I resolved with all my heart that his assassins, after stamping out his life, would not succeed in stamping out his ideas, too." On the foundation's logo is a bicycle whose front light is on, illuminating the street.

In the fall of 2006, Marina Orlandi felt an old fear coming back. Her instincts placed her on alert. The slogans at recent protest marches were taking on a tone she knew all too well, reminiscent of the public lynching of her husband. So she broke her own rule and ended her silence by writing a public message on the occasion of the inauguration of the Marco Biagi Foundation's new offices at the University of Modena. "Whenever we try to address the labor issues, we end up exacerbating a conflict that quickly degenerates into a debate that is not only sterile but, as unfortunately we know all too well, extremely dangerous." Her commitment to defending the memory of her husband is unwavering, even if she does so mostly in silence and without appearing in public. She doesn't allow herself to be photographed, and she defends her children's and her own privacy because she wants to continue to walk freely through the streets of Bologna.

When slander is repeated insistently enough, it creates an entirely new person that supplants the old. I cannot help but think back on my father and the way he was portrayed between 1969 and 1972, with the collusion of newspapers, plays, films, leaflets, and graffiti (some of which seems to have survived the passage of time, as well as the denials and the proof). Today we are still obliged to read that Luigi Calabresi·was trained in America, that he was in the CIA, that in 1966 he was the official escort of the American general Edwin A. Walker, and that it was he who introduced Walker to General Giovanni De Lorenzo, who was organizing a coup d'état in Italy. Yet it would take so little, the tiniest speck of intelligence or curiosity, a minimum of fact-checking, to disprove these claims. My father didn't speak a word of English and never had the possibility to learn it or the time to travel. The only stamp on his passport was issued in Barcelona on May 31, 1969: the first day of the honeymoon that took my parents to Granada and Seville, where I was conceived. Then, he went to Switzerland on business. Nowhere else. Never crossed the ocean. This could all be disputed, to the greater joy of the conspiracy theorists, were it not for one small detail: the facts. He graduated from college in 1965. He applied to become deputy chief inspector, and in 1966 he attended the training courses at the policemen's academy. It would be beyond belief for the CIA to assign Rome to a fresh graduate, to assign him to escort a general around Rome, or for a student at the police academy to act as the intermediary between the Americans and an Italian general planning a coup. Recently I looked into who this General Walker was: he was an American general who fought in Italy in World War II and then in Korea; he leaned so far to the right that the Secretary of Defense under Kennedy, Robert McNamara, removed him from his post and he left the army. In 1961.

My father sued *Lotta Continua* for accusing him of being Pinelli's murderer and for the American "legends" it had concocted, in the hope of demonstrating that the accusations against him were libelous. It was a suit that my mother opposed until the end—"You're playing their game"—but my father explained that he had been asked to file suit by the Ministry of the Interior. It was a waste of time and the trial backfired, becoming an opportunity for his enemies to recycle all their libelous attacks on him. In the end, the judge was recused and the trial was suspended and assigned to other judges. It did not come to an end until four years after my father's death, when the editor in chief of *Lotta Continua* was convicted of libel.

After the recusal, eight hundred intellectuals signed a document published in *L'espresso* on June 13, 1971, in which my father was called "Inspector Torture" and "responsible for the demise of Pinelli." The list of signatories was endless. I've met dozens of them over the years, although I've only talked about the document with one, Lucio Colletti. I met him at the Montecitorio Palace when, his Marxist days long over, he was a Member of Parliament for Forza Italia. I would buy him a coffee, and he would offer me one of those thin cigarettes he was always smoking, then he'd give me a few choice quotes for whatever piece I was writing. In 2001, when the election ballots were being drawn up, I did a humorous interview with him in which he took aim at his own party, calling them lily-livered softies. He said he was going to cash in his chips and retire. They took him at his word and took his name off the ballot. The next day he called me, feeling a little down, and said, "You ruined me. You know I can't resist a good joke and you got me. But what can I say. After all, I do feel like I owe you something. *Pazienza!* I guess I'll have to look for a bench in the sun." That afternoon I saw Berlusconi in the Transatlantico Room at the Montecitorio Palace. I followed him and said, "Do you really want to act like a Stalinist and kick someone out for a remark that was meant to be funny? It's my fault. Colletti was joking." In the end, they put his name back on the slate, and he was ready to make fun of Berlusconi and his cohorts all over again.

• • •

In the July 3, 2002, issue of *Corriere della Sera*, the former editor in chief, Paolo Mieli (he would return to the paper's helm in December 2004), replied to a letter on the subject of universities and specialized degrees. Referring to the long list of signatures affixed to the bottom of the letter, he took the opportunity to say something that had evidently been on his mind for some time. The title of his reply was "Beware of Signatures at the Bottom of Petitions and Manifestos." I have the clipping in a large envelope in the center drawer of a seventeenth-century bureau bought at an auction at the charterhouse of Pavia in 1969. It was the prize piece of my parents' house on Via Cherubini. On the left side of the drawer are thousands of letters collected in colored files. On the right is the envelope with letters to the editor or articles that have a special meaning.

Mieli wrote:

I wish to object, with all due respect, to the form of your protest. "I have a great dislike for public petitions, for any type of petition. Because I consider them, in the best of cases, useless and sometimes ridiculous, almost always tainted with identifiable outbursts of exhibitionism. To sign this type of sheet costs nothing, absolutely nothing. Despite the gladiatorial tones that abound in these petitions, it takes no courage to adhere to one. On the contrary. Let me add that many years ago my signature ended up (mea culpa) at the bottom of one of these protests. It was the promoters' intention, and mine, that this appeal serve as a step in favor of freedom of the press, but due to a reprehensible ambiguity in its formulation, the text gave the impression of defending the armed struggle and encouraging the lynching of Luigi Calabresi. Shortly thereafter the inspector was killed and I, some thirty years later, am still ashamed of that coincidence. As I believe (or at least I hope) are all those whose names appeared at the bottom of that sheet. Ashamed is the least I can say: any word of apol-

ogy to the wife and children of Luigi Calabresi seems inadequate in view of the gravity of this episode. I am quite famil-
iar, as I said, with how signatures end up on this type of
petition. Sometimes you get a hasty phone call. But often the
people directly concerned know nothing about it. The Greek
writer Vassilis Vassilikos—the author of the book on which the
film *Z* was based, which evoked the events leading up to the
coup d'état by the colonels in Athens—tells the story of how
in 1967, a few days after the coup, he read in *Le Monde* a petition by seventy French intellectuals requesting his own immediate release. "I was having an espresso at a sidewalk café
underneath the Roman sun and I became alarmed," he recalls.
"I immediately phoned Gallimard, my publishing house, to tell
them that I was safe and sound abroad and that I would soon
be in Paris." But the surprise did not end there. Two months
later, when he arrived in the French capital, he contacted some
of the people who had signed the petition and discovered that
none of them knew they had signed. Ultimately Marguerite
Duras explained what had happened: everyone had delegated
their signatures as a blank check to Jean-Paul Sartre and Simone
de Beauvoir. When Sartre and his wife decided to protest something, their action automatically included the signatures of the
other sixty-eight. Vassilikos at least had the courage to tell the
tale and the honesty to joke about it.

From the same envelope, I take out a letter from Folco Quilici,
written in 1991, and a paid advertisement published on May 18,
1997, in the left-wing newspaper *Manifesto*. In the letter, Quilici,
a writer and documentarian famous for his works on the sea,
describes how he discovered that his signature was among the
eight hundred. "Dear Signora Calabresi, I wanted to tell you that
it was not me. I have the feeling that it was someone else or that
my signature was added without contacting me. Indeed, please
believe me when I say how saddened I am by the assassination

of a man of courage." The newspaper clipping instead comes from people who were on the other front: it is a short communiqué prepared on the occasion of the twenty-fifth anniversary of my father's death. At the bottom there are eleven signatures, all from former leaders of Lotta Continua.

> On the anniversary of that crime for which our friends Adriano Sofri, Ovidio Bompressi, and Giorgio Pietrostefani, who we know are innocent, are incarcerated, we—who in the past shared ideas, words, and behaviors—feel that it is our duty to recognize that before his murder, Luigi Calabresi was subject to a political and press campaign that went beyond the limits of resolute protest and that aroused sentiments of hatred toward him that helped to create the climate that led to his assassination. That campaign and those sentiments cannot be justified, then or now, not even by our sense of duty to denounce the abuses committed in the investigations into the Piazza Fontana massacre and demand the truth about the murder of Giuseppe Pinelli. There is no excuse for the way many of us welcomed the news of the killing of Luigi Calabresi: not one word was expended on the value of a human life, even that of an adversary, nor on the grievous violence that the killing of a man does to his family members.

The signatories include Nini Briglia, who today is the director of the periodicals division of Mondadori. Briglia and I have never met, but I did telephone him to find out how this letter came about. "It was a difficult path: at the beginning there were many of us but in the end only eleven signed. The initiative was born from the desire to take a step forward, to question and face up to the tragic reality of those years. At the same time, however, we felt a strong bond with our friends, and did not want to damage their defense. The negotiations went on forever. There were some of us that wanted a more unequivocal statement, while others resisted. The end product is a hybrid that in my opinion is unsatisfactory. But it was a step forward and it was better than nothing." The fact that I have kept it in the file in the drawer of the seventeenth-century bureau means that it was indeed better than nothing.

One of the signatories of the communiqué was Caterina's grandmother, the famous novelist Natalia Ginzburg. For me she was always the author of *Family Sayings*, which our elementary school teacher used to read out loud in class. Caterina's uncle, Carlo Ginzburg, wrote one of the best-known essays in defense of Adriano Sofri, *The Judge and the Historian*. The second time that Caterina and I went out together, on a summer afternoon in Rome, we asked each other almost in unison, "Are our family differences a problem for you?" "No, not at all," we both answered at the same time. One evening before our wedding, the prominent leftist Vittorio Foa and his wife, Sesa, invited us to their house. They had prepared *gnocchi al pomodoro*, as was the custom at the Ginzburg house, and Vittorio told Caterina, "This is a dinner that your grandmother would have prepared. *In bocca al lupo*—good luck!" Today we have two little girls, twins, who were born in New York and have both our family names: Emma and Irene Calabresi-Ginzburg. Their passports with two names that have become one are clear proof that they belong to the new century.

Many times at the office of *La Repubblica*, after we had finished putting the newspaper to bed, I would stop by to see the editor in chief, Ezio Mauro. We would talk for hours about the 1970s and terrorism. His lucid views always impressed me. "Being a reporter in Turin during the first years of terrorism helped me to understand things that others could grasp only much later through deduction. I saw them unfolding right in front of me. All you had to do was go to the house of a prison guard who had been shot and meet the young wife with a child in her arms: even an idiot would have realized that the Red Brigades had to be stopped. I remember Antonio Cocozzello, an elementary school teacher and Christian Democrat councilman who had come to Turin from the Basilicata region. They shot him in the legs at a streetcar stop in the fall of 1977. He slid to the ground along the pole of a street sign and stayed there for a long time waiting for the ambulance. I made it in time to observe him and see the humble clothes he was wearing, and on the ground a plastic folder holding files for the fund of CISL, a trade union with strong ties to the Christian Democrats. He was helping people get their pensions. I went back to the *Gazzetta del Popolo*, where I found the terrorists' claims: 'We have lamed a Christian Democrat leader.' I was well aware of what Christian Democrat power was and I didn't like it at all, but right then and there I realized that Cocozzello had nothing to do with that power and that the Red Brigades were not on the side of the people and the poor. I went home and wrote sixty pages for my friends that I rediscovered a few years ago. In them I called the state an empty shell and asked, 'But if we lose that shell, the democratic institutions, what will we have left?'"

Cocozzello was shot by Patrizio Peci, who later became the first Red Brigade turncoat. I was with Ezio one afternoon in early September 2002 when he called Peppe D'Avanzo, who was interviewing Peci, twenty years after the death of Carlo Alberto Dalla Chiesa. Peppe wanted him to describe how Dalla Chiesa had convinced him to repent and had succeeded in crippling the Red Brigades. Peppe passed the phone to Peci, whose opening remark was "Signor Mauro, do you still drive an orange Renault?" Ezio was shocked and replied no. It seems that he had been tailed for a long time and that the Red Brigades had been thinking of targeting him rather than Carlo Casalegno, the journalist whom they killed in 1977. Mauro was much younger and less important, but he wrote editorials on terrorism and did not have an escort.

Ezio's tales of the city and of its biggest industry, the Fiat automobile manufacturer, are filled with civic passion. "As Gianni Agnelli used to say, those who haven't lived in Turin cannot understand what terrorism was like: because of the intensity of it all, people stopped going out at night, and in the morning they would turn on the radio to hear who had been shot. The only time that I cried was when the great journalist Walter Tobagi was murdered. I was in front of the TV in the newsroom. It followed the same pattern: acts of violence and attempts to get the factory riled up. In this case, the factory workers didn't take the bait, except for some fringe elements. I remember the words of Pietro Ingrao, a senior figure in the Italian Communist party, after the death of Casalegno. 'You cannot kill in the name of the working class, in the name of ideology. You who have waged a union struggle for one hundred years to improve the life of a man by one quarter of an hour, how can you then have him murdered?' During the years of terrorism the Italian Communist Party defended the government institutions: it had many shortcomings and many faults, but its defense of the government was not one of them."

Judge Guido Salvini has just finished explaining to me his inquest into the death of Antonio Custra, the young policeman who died in the shootout on Via De Amicis in Milan on May 17, 1977. We speak briefly about my father, about Lotta Continua in Milan, the Piazza Fontana massacre, and the death of Pinelli. I stand up, thank him, and am on my way out the door when he clears his throat and says, betraying a certain tension, "Please, Calabresi, have a seat for another moment." I was speechless. I turned around and did what he asked, looking at him inquisitively. "When your father died, I was seventeen years old.

I was a young militant, although I was a Socialist, and I, too, shouted those slogans on the streets. Yes, the slogans that you know well, you understand what I mean. Well, I wanted to tell you that I am ashamed, and I apologize to you and to your mother. For myself I can only ask for your forgiveness. We said things without thinking. We could not imagine the violence they would cause. There is only one thing that gives me peace. When your father was killed, I was not among those that celebrated, nor even among those who spouted conspiracy theories. I felt sick to my stomach about what had happened." My throat closed from the emotion, and I thanked him. I stood up and left the courthouse.

breathe

IN APRIL 2000, I was offered a job at *La Repubblica* by the then editor of the political section, Massimo Giannini, and his deputy, Giorgio Casada. I had been working for five years at the ANSA wire service, and I dreamed of transferring to a daily newspaper. I liked the proposal, but one thing about it made me very uncomfortable: Could I work for a newspaper that published the articles of Adriano Sofri? I thought about it for a few days, saying nothing at home, but the rumor began to circulate. One day I was stopped at the Transatlantico Room at Montecitorio Palace by the spokesman for one of the center-left leaders, who said to me mysteriously, "Your father is turning over in his grave."

I took the train to Milan. My mother as usual served us coffee in the orange-bordered cups, the last souvenir of our apartment on Via Cherubini. I told her about the job offer and said that I was thinking of turning it down. She amazed me once again with her freshness and insight. She calmly asked me a series of questions: "Is it a good job? Do you like it? Is it a promotion? Are there people that you can learn from?" I answered yes to every question, but cautiously. So she added one final question. "If Sofri didn't publish there, would you have any doubts?" No, I would almost certainly go, I replied. She smiled and said, "So go, then. Don't listen to anyone, relax. I knew your father better than anyone, and I'm sure he would have said the same thing. He loved challenges, confrontation, mixing with people. In his head there weren't two Italys, just one." Then she looked at me. I was still confused, so she added what was perhaps closest to her heart. "Mario, don't let other people decide your fate. They already did it once when you were a child. This time you be the one to decide."

I signed the contract. Some people were perplexed, but no one said anything to me about it, until November 2005, when at a high school ceremony to commemorate the victims of the Years of Lead, the speaker asked me out of the blue: How can you work for *La Repubblica*, where Sofri also writes? I answered with a joke. "If that's the criterion, then there are not many papers I could work for in Italy . . . maybe I should change professions."

I remember one Sunday with Silvio Berlusconi at Santa Margherita Ligure. I managed to get an interview from him on the street, the only kind he would allow. I had just started working at *La Stampa* after a year at *La Repubblica*. I find him by the seaside, getting out of a car together with his daughter Marina. They buy a few things and then get an ice cream. I tag along. At every store we enter, Berlusconi says hello and then repeats the same lines. "Do you see this boy? He would be a great journalist but last year he became a Communist . . . unfortunately, he works for *La Repubblica*." He says it once, twice, three times. I play along with it, smiling, limiting myself to saying, "Cavaliere, life is unpredictable: you can become a Communist without realizing it, even in the twenty-first century." Then at every exit I ask him another question for the interview. At the fifth store, a pharmacy, one of the clerks makes a face when she hears "*La*

Repubblica" and looks at me suspiciously. I feel like a stranger in a strange land, and the whole thing seems truly grotesque. I've been coming to this town for years, to the beach, to dinner, to the discotheques, summer and winter. I felt at home until a few moments ago. Can a label suddenly change who I really am? To tell the truth, Berlusconi was quick to accept my working for an opposition paper. A few months earlier, he had agreed to grant me and *La Repubblica* the interview in which he revealed that he had had a bout with cancer, but I have never forgotten the reaction of that pharmacist.

The important thing, I have always thought, is to be yourself, to be faithful to your ideas, to respect your own history. Then you can have peace of mind anywhere you go. Almost anywhere.

I have a sixth sense. There are situations when at a certain point I perceive something in the air that tells me to leave. I remember an evening in 1992, at a party. I don't like the atmosphere, I don't like the conversation. I am on pins and needles until I overhear a sentence. They're talking about my mother. I take a breath and stop to listen. A woman is speaking. "It's so disgusting. They gave all this money to the widow and she plays the victim, talking, talking." She adds, laughing, "They should have killed her, too."

I hold my breath for a few seconds, perfectly still, like a stone. Something inside me dies. I have only enough breath to say nine words very slowly and in a low voice. "I don't think that's exactly the way things are."

"What do you know?"

I look her in the eyes. I don't have the energy to argue, or maybe instead I'm afraid that I won't be able to control myself. So I am discreet. "The money. She didn't get very much. She became an elementary school teacher to take care of her children."

"How do you know?"

"She's my mother."

No one says a word. The seconds ticking by seem like an eternity. The woman turns beet red, looking for words she cannot find. I feel faint. I look for the hostess, say good night, and thank her. I make it to the door, go out into the humid Milanese winter, and search for air. My head is pounding.

"I struggle to keep all these things far from my heart, to forget them, not to focus on the rudeness, the insults, to be able to look to the future, to avoid being embittered." Mama is speaking on the telephone. I'm telling her about the boxes filled with paper that I want to throw away, the hurtful sentences that I've found in the newspaper clippings, all the things we have had to digest. "How did you manage?" I ask her.

"I staked my bets on life. What else could I do at the age of twenty-five with two little children to take care of and a third on the way? I kept busy every day, the only antidote for depression, and I tried to inoculate myself against giving in to laziness, to hatred, to becoming an angry victim. This doesn't mean you should be docile or put your head in the sand. It means you should fight for truth and justice and continue to live, renewing the memory every day. To do otherwise would mean giving in completely to the terrorists, and handing a victory to their culture of death."

The sons of Marina Orlandi Biagi were twelve and nineteen when their father was killed. They are big boys with open friendly faces, smiling, making plans, traveling, arguing. It's miraculous that she was able to keep them going, to push them toward the future. Marina protects them, but she has never constructed easy truths or given into despondency, and she keeps alive the lesson that their father had taught them: "Marco used to say that even though they were young, they should feel like an active, integral part of society, and that they already had great responsibilities. He would tell them that they were good boys, in order to prepare them to be good men. He used to tell them to always seek truth and justice, without worrying about being unpopular, to take the side of the weak and reject the violent." Marina has no intention of giving in to despair or anger, and while she is speaking I see my mother and many other widows from the Years of Lead. "The terrorists struck my family with an unacceptable cruelty, but they did not succeed in taking away our life force."

Twenty-five years after the death of Tobagi, Giampaolo Pansa wrote of how he was summoned to give a deposition at the 1983 trial where he met Stella, the journalist's widow.

> Stella spoke to me at length. One of the things that she said has stuck in my mind: she told me that she was trying to raise Luca and Benedetta without hatred for anyone. I left the bunker of that trial humbled by her equanimity. Not long after, I read an interview with Stella in *Corriere*, and I found the words that I had heard in the witness-box. "My children are perfectly aware of what happened. I have always told them everything, they know everything. And I think I've succeeded in freeing them from any feeling of rancor or hatred."
>
> As for me, there is one thing I am certain of: those awful years changed all of us for the worse. They made us more hard-hearted, more brutal in our anxiety to forget, to erase the shadows of the dead and even the faces of those who are still alive. I often hear people say that we did too little to protect the militants and the gunmen. I don't know if that's really true. What I do know for certain is that we were inhumane with the wives, the children, and the parents of those who were killed.

For a long time, I oscillated between my mother's lesson and a blunt desire to take out my anger on everyone. When the talk began about clemency, I was shocked. I felt uncentered, without any fixed point to hold on to. Then I came up with the idea of going to the mountains, of looking for the place deep in the Valle d'Aosta where my grandfather had taught me to ski. For days and days, he had worked on it: lessons with a coach in the morning, and practice with him in the afternoon. He seemed to be rushing me, until he said, "Now I think you're ready to ski the Val Veny trail."

The descent through the woods rewards you with a complete panorama of the Mont Blanc chain. In front of the Brenva Glacier, he straightened his coarse wool cap, took off his gloves, and put in his mouth a Baratti rhubarb candy, which he always kept in his pocket. Then he started to talk to me and I realized that all those lessons had a single goal, to bring me to this place. "When your father died, I looked for him for a long time. Then one day when I was here by myself, I found him, and every time I come back I feel him. I wanted you to know." He said nothing more and I remained in silence. Three years later, Grandfather died from a stroke, before the trials had begun.

That morning I went up on the first ski lift, the one taken by the ski masters in red ski jackets. The trails were still pure and the snow squeaked beneath my skis. When I made it to the point where you can see the rock wall of Aiguille Noire de Peutérey, which cuts across the summit of Mont Blanc, I was completely alone. Standing still with my eyes staring at the ice, I found first my grandfather, then Papà Gigi. I stood there for a long time listening to him, and I felt that it was right to look forward, to move, to commit to opening a new chapter out of respect for his memory. I had to carry him into the world with me, not humiliate him with arguments and rage, if I did not want to betray him. I had to place my bets on life and on love.

acknowledgments

I have a debt of gratitude to four friends who assisted the birth of this book.

Filippo Ceccarelli read it and discussed it with the passion and scrupulousness that are the hallmark of his life and work.

With Gianni Riotta, I have for years walked down the street in the evening talking about the 1970s, terrorism, and the need for me to write what I feel. He encouraged me and supported this project every time I was tempted to put it on the back burner.

Luigi Contu and Michele Fusco were always there every time that the tempests of politics and journalism were unleashed on my family. They helped me to react, to reflect, and to choose how I wanted to respond. Their advice has always been precious and their presence has given me the gift of serenity.

index